The Bread of Salt and Other Stories

The Bread of Salt

and

Other Stories

N. V. M. GONZALEZ

University of Washington Press

Seattle & London

Library of Congress Cataloging-in-Publication Data
González, N. V. M., 1915–
   The bread of salt and other stories / N. V. M. González.
    p.   cm.
   ISBN 0-295-97246-7
   1. Philippines—Fiction.   I. Title.
PR9550.9.G66B7   1993   92-43922
823—dc20   CIP

For Narita

Contents

CONTENTS

viii

Preface

MORE THAN TWENTY-FOUR YEARS AND MANY dreams ago, I arrived in Santa Barbara, California, to begin what would become a long sojourn in America. A family friend, an Irish American Jesuit, had read in *Time* magazine about the lifestyle of Californians; but he was confident I would know what was best. He would have been alarmed had he realized that I was not unlike my narrator in "Crossing Over," who arrives with a pinstripe woolen suit, a gift from an uncle in the merchant marine, for his first winter in America. He makes it to Oakland. Then, amidst imagined hazards, he finds his way to the Southern Pacific train station, in San Francisco, on Townsend and Third. My situation was the same, except that as a hedge against the future I had brought along several short stories, two novels, and various scraps of writing.

This was of course quixotic, considering that my writings were peopled with subsistence farmers in their barefoot dignity and fishermen daring the seas in their frail outriggers. My inventory included, too, those whom Nabokov calls "puppets of memory," the companions of my childhood and youth—schoolteachers and their pupils, maidservants and their mistresses or masters, college dropouts, small-town merchants—the underclass who constitute the majority in all societies.

Some of them were in my first book of short stories, *Seven Hills Away* (1947), and I am certain that my coming to America on a writing fellowship two years later was their handiwork. So how can I not be grateful to each and every one of them? And grateful, for good measure, to Mindoro, the scene of their labors, that "poor island with a wondrous name," as the *Philippines Free Press* once said.

A discalced Franciscan must have put me to it. He wrote of Mindoro ever so long ago as an island "shaped like the heart and located in the centre of the archipelago called Filipinas." The other islands bear to it the same relation, he said, "as the various parts of the body do to the heart." Clearly, here was my metaphor.

But what a struggle lay ahead. My idols of the forties, almost every one, had held a proud and writerly disregard for formal education. That, thought I, was precisely the way to go. Having won, with *Seven Hills Away*, a fellowship year in America, I would forgo pursuing a diploma; I would design instead a study program of my own.

At Stanford, where I began my American year, my classmates were reading Henry James. For my part, I toiled away to re-create Mindoro. It took exactly twenty-two drafts of "A Warm Hand" before I managed to set the maid Elay upon the deck of the *batel* "Ligaya," the wind upon her face. Forthwith, I introduced her to Katherine Anne Porter, herself an autodidact, who was on the teaching staff that academic quarter. It was she who urged me to send Elay's story to *Sewanee Review*. I could not have been more confident of the future.

Not till many years later would I meet again, one evening in San Francisco, my Stanford professor Wallace Stegner. The Wheatland Foundation had organized that summer a conference on world literature, and over seventy writers had come from all over. Professor and Mrs. Stegner had been invited to the inaugural dinner and, to me, this gave the event a grand design attributable to none other than the Fates.

At his avuncular best, and with the warmth and sincerity that have sent many of us hurrying back to the workbench,

Mr. Stegner asked me about the novel I had been working on while at the Stanford Writing Center. That was forty years ago! So he did remember! I have written two others, said I, rather in self-defense, adding quickly that I would soon go back to that early project.

Maybe the time had come to be heard. We were too close, though, to events in Europe, and the conference turned out to be somewhat Eurocentric. Sadly missing, in particular, was any interest in Southeast Asia. When asked if he were acquainted with writing from the Philippines, an East German poet replied, curiously enough, that he did not feel compelled anyhow to read literature except for pleasure. "You have to seduce us," he said, which drew murmurs of delight from the audience. From my seat in the next-to-the-last row, I said: "Ah, but one must see the lady first in order to be seduced."

A week later I was sent a copy of a London *Economist* article on the conference—coming full circle, I thought, since the correspondent had been my student at California State University, Hayward. The article carried, not unwittingly perhaps, the title "Alas, Alack. . . ."

I did receive a not indelicate reward for one small seduction. From a Chinese anthology editor came a mooncake about the size of a dinner plate for translation rights to "The Blue Skull and the Dark Palms." Soviet editors did even better later on; they brought out ten stories, together with the novel *A Season of Grace*. Dewan Bahasa Dan Pustaka, the Malaysian publishing house, followed with the same novel in translation.

Small triumphs, at the most; but something has happened. Frank O'Connor has been proved right. An audience out there has found the "submerged population" about whom he spoke. This is the stuff of short stories, although there may appear various aspects of it "from writer to writer, from generation to generation"—and from country to country, I must hasten to add. In the Philippines, colonization made us into a truly submerged people. We are not mere fictions.

To write fictions about us would seem superfluous and irrelevant, were it not for the fact that Art intervenes even as we attempt to give form to our judgment. With English, which America brought to the country initially as a tool for colonial administration, came a tradition and a culture ready to hand.

The language has been with us for nine decades now. While these have been years of grieving over fancied or real losses in the native culture, these have also been years of opportune expression through a borrowed language. An alien language does not fail if it is employed in honest service to the scene, in evocation of the landscape, and in celebration of the people one has known from birth.

This prospect, though, acquired its own dimension; it revealed, even, its own history. The imagined and the factual had to be blocked off, one from the other, the fictional from the workaday: this was the discipline to observe. To gird off "A Shelter of Bamboo and Sand" and thereby to express the ineffable, a soldier in the Philippine American war, a black man, crosses over to the Filipino side at San Miguel de Mayumo. So as not to be taken for the enemy, he rolls up his shirt sleeve and bares his arm there in the dark. Here, I thought, is the first of the three wars of my deigesis, the world to which all my stories can relate—should a reader care to relate them to history.

Many discrete items—the Longfellow poem and the magazine covers in "The Lives of Great Men"; the twilight hours in "The Gecko and the Mermaid"; the boy's sun-baked head of hair smelling like a basket of dried anchovies, after a morning spent in the sun, in "The Long Harvest"—these, singly and together, may seem to come in the order of found objects from some beach front awash with random experience. But this is no perversity; rather, only a further aspect of the grammar of our lives.

For there is a conspiracy these days against the creative act: Time mounts it upon our best intentions, flouting even our sincerest hopes. No method can accommodate the future. Those ubiquitous rolls of the Filipino breakfast table, the *pan de sal,* make this case for us. When I wrote "The Bread of Salt," the *pan de sal* was usually the size of one's fist. Until then, no emblem gave me more confidence or a greater joy. Today, it brings on a subdued sadness, for these rolls have shrunk to the miserable size of a chicken's egg. Who can say whether, in a year or two, the *pan de sal* won't be just a wee bit larger than a quail's egg. Is the meaning thereby degraded?

Contingencies such as these do not seem to work on the writer's behalf in the fictions we construct. Maybe that is just as well, since fiction has an autonomy of its own. Still, we must ask whether Time's capacity for betrayal has urged the boy Roberto Cruz, in "The Wireless Tower," to seek his own sort of truth, and whether it has indeed designed a career for Professor Leynes, in "The Popcorn Man," provost at a College of the Doomed, whose alumni are scattered far and wide.

I must confess to an admiration for the Professor. Maybe only to his kind do the Fates vouchsafe a vision of one's country. He and Nonong Padua in "The Long Harvest," if a generation apart, are possibly alike, although for Nonong the chipmunks and crested bluejays at Padelford do suggest a victory of sorts. And this is heartening: we should not list metonymy among the unemployed.

A new situation is upon us, after all. Owing to economic turmoil and political upheavals, Filipinos have become a diaspora of unprecedented proportions. Understandably, America has become the destination of choice. Still, there is probably no place in the world that Filipinos have not strayed into and wandered about, yielding to a restlessness and a seeking that has long been on record.

In an 1883 article in *Harper's Weekly*, Lafcadio Hearn describes how "Manila men" did themselves proud, building a Visayan village in the bayou country of Louisiana. Are voyages and journeys all that Fortune can offer us? I find, going by my own kind of reckoning, that "The Sea Beyond" gives us a young wife's beginning, and "Come and Go" gives us a wanderer's pause. For arrivals and departures, consider the old man in "The Tomato Game," and Mrs. Bilbao in "Where's My Baby Now?" As for Mr. Malto's landlady in "The Whispering Woman," she is quick to note, in the quiet of a Buenavista evening, how taps is sounded "all the way from across town." To sum it up, our sailor in "The Morning Star" falls back on an utterance that consists of but one syllable: "Ha!" His seems as close to optimism and hope as the language allows. But he belongs to the story; we can hardly claim such sage imperturbability for ourselves.

There is in *Webster's Third New International Dictionary* an entry well worth looking up: *kaingin,* the Tagalog word for "swidden." Mindoro is, even to this day, kaingin country. The dictionary quotes Wallace Stegner: "some lonely farmer hewing out a — in the jungle."

"Kaingin" happens also to be the title I gave a poem, one of my earliest, published in the *Philippine Magazine*. More than anybody else in the country in the thirties and forties, its editor, A. V. H. Hartendorp, held highest hopes for a Filipino literature in English. He was among the few who felt proud over the occasional attention paid our writing by the late Edward J. O'Brien, an outstanding critic of the American and British short story. O'Brien's notice, while by no means considerable, came without hype or the carrot of patronage, and it helped an entire generation of Filipino writers to aspire.

In April, I shall be in the kaingin,

the poem began, unsure of its language and uncertain in its direction. By happenstance it took me to the right stop, and in more ways than I had intended:

> I shall scamper from one log
> > to another;
> In the worsening heat
> Some palm tree I shall seek;
> I shall pick my steps upon the ash-covered
> > ground,
> Then make my way
> To the edge of the clearing,
> To a murmuring stream.
> There I shall wash
> The ashes from my feet.

The poem found its way to Washington, D.C. How, I never learned. And why? To prove something, perhaps. In any event, a generous editor stuck it onto a corner of a page in a Department of Education publication.

There followed a solid block of time. The ash-covered loam of the forest clearing joined a park bench in Seattle, in "The Long Harvest," to serve as its frame. And at the center of these years, an eighteen-year-old graduate from the Philippine Normal School took a brief posting in Romblon, a copra-trading town, followed by a transfer to Mindoro, for work as a school district supervisor and weekend homesteader. It was a move not unlike one from a provincial capital to the sticks; and as a search for Fortune, it was as challenging. For thirteen more years, Father pursued this divided life, abandoning school service altogether as he glimpsed great prospects in copra and hemp. To his first-born, he would leave, and not untrustingly, the world beyond the clearing.

I began to write straight out of high school, innocently turning to the English-language weeklies as an alternative to job-seeking in Manila, where everyone went to escape the poverty of the provinces. My first writings appeared in the early 1930s. All the while, Father's efforts at planting coconut and abaca, raising cattle, even cutting and selling lumber came to naught. He had worked, while a schoolboy, in the household of one of the Thomasites and, without his knowing it, had become one of the intermediaries of the new order and dispensation. As an unintended premium, his son could recite Longfellow at the drop of a hat. Then came the Depression, and with it just the appropriate sharpness of the blade to whittle aspirations to manageable size.

It is perhaps possible to assign "Kaingin" as Father's first harvest, along with those stories in *Philippine Magazine* that, in 1947, were collected to become *Seven Hills Away*. Father was their first reader. How avidly he followed Tarang's progress from draft to draft until, two years later, there emerged "Children of the Ash-Covered Loam." Tarang's stubbing of his big toe upon a tree stump could have been Father's own primal experience, his own seeing anew of some other kaingin being restored to the forest, to "the dark womb of the land at this time of night."

This really had never occurred to me till now. Indeed, till now, despite my passing six and seventy, I had not understood that there had been played out, in Father's very experience, literally and incontrovertibly, the interaction of Filipino and American cultures. When historians talk about Manifest Destiny, about "special relationships" and all that, it is also of him that they must speak. And it is this that I had failed to see; it may well be that he took this lived history as a given, leaving us the task of making some sense out of it.

It is simply difficult to say where dreams begin. But in our title story, Robert Louis Stevenson's *The Sire de Maletroit's Door* left our class "enthralled," our breaths "trembling." A memorial, however modest, is in order, something worthy of those years. For a start, at the very least, stories can provide the gift of remembering.

Alan Swallow published my first book of short stories, *Seven Hills Away*, in 1947; twelve tales of the Philippines, he called them. Though none of the twelve are in this collection, for reasons of space and thematic unity, I have included some from the *Selected Stories* that he brought out in 1964. The present collection may be considered a retrospective, not only of my work but also of the kindnesses of the pioneers who have made it possible—the University of the Philippines Press, Benipayo, Bookmark, and New Day Publishers—whose generous offices will long be remembered. It is to these, and to other enterprising presses in the Philippines, that many a Filipino writer is indebted for saving his material from the scrap heap of old magazines and periodicals and for allowing it the dignity of bookcovers.

The interest and support of the University of Washington Press over the last few years must not go unacknowledged. I note it with boundless gratefulness. When it became known that I had been ill, the editor's letters that reached me in Diliman, in the Philippines, or in Hayward, were not only queries about my progress in putting together these stories but also about my health. When a letter failed to find me at one address, there was always a thoughtful friend around who knew where to find me. How does one properly express one's gratitude for such concern and encouragement? Indeed, in preparing the manuscript for this collection, I came away wondering over the world's kindness to my work. Perhaps only by writing still more can I begin to pay that back.

I have included here, meanwhile, four stories that are not to be found in any collection. In tone and subject matter, they might suggest coming full circle—in the learning of one's craft, in finding a language, and, finally, in discovering a country of one's own.

Los Angeles
California

Eight of these stories first appeared in the volume *Children of the Ash-Covered Loam* (Manila: Benipayo, 1954); six were published in *Look, Stranger, on this Island Now* (Manila: Benipayo, 1963). All the preceding, plus seven others (including "The Lives of Great Men," first published in the Philippines *Free Press*, October 30, 1964; and "The Tomato Game" first published in *Asia Philippines Leader*, June 16, 1972), appeared in *Mindoro and Beyond: Twenty-One Stories* (Quezon City: University of the Philippines Press, 1979), and were copyrighted 1979 by N. V. M. Gonzalez. Four from the first volume appeared in *Selected Stories* (Denver, Colorado: Alan Swallow, 1964) and were copyrighted 1964 by N. V. M. Gonzalez. "In the Twilight" first appeared in *Mindoro and Beyond*. "Crossing Over," from the Philippines *Daily Express*, "This Week

Magazine," July 18, 1982; "A Shelter of Bamboo and Sand," from *National Midweek Magazine*, December 7, 1982; "The Gecko and the Mermaid," from *Amerasia Journal*, IV:2 (1988); and "The Long Harvest," from *National Midweek Magazine*, May 23, 1990, appear here in a collection for the first time.

The Bread of Salt and Other Stories

A Warm Hand

HOLDING ON TO THE RIGGING, ELAY LEANED OVER.
The dinghy was being readied. The wind tore her hair into
wiry strands that fell across her face, heightening her aware-
ness of the dipping and rising of the deck. But for the bite
of the *noroeste,* she would have begun to feel faint and empty
in her belly. Now she clutched at the rigging with more
courage.

At last the dinghy shoved away with its first load of passengers—seven boys from Bongabon, Mindoro, on their way
to Manila to study. The deck seemed less hostile than before,
for the boys had made a boisterous group then; now that
they were gone, her mistress Ana could leave the crowded
deckhouse for once.

"Oh, Elay! My powder puff!"

It was Ana, indeed. Elay was familiar with that excitement which her mistress wore about her person like a silk
kerchief—now on her head to keep her hair in place, now
like a scarf round her neck. How eager Ana had been to go
ashore when the old skipper of the *batel* said that the *Ligaya*
was too small a boat to brave the coming storm. She must
return to the deckhouse, Elay thought, if she must fetch her
mistress's handbag.

With both hands upon the edge of the deckhouse roof, she
bent forward and came abreast of the wooden water barrel
to the left of the main mast. From there she staggered back
to the deckhouse entrance. As she bent her head low lest
with the lurching of the boat her brow should hit the door
frame, she saw her mistress on all fours clambering out of the

3

deckhouse. She let her have the right-of-way, entering only after Ana was safe upon the open deck.

Elay found the handbag—she was certain that the powder puff would be there—though not without difficulty, inside the canvas satchel that she meant to take ashore. She came dragging the heavy satchel, and in a flurry Ana dug into it for the bag. The deck continued to sway, yet presently Ana was powdering her face; and this done, she applied lipstick to that full, round mouth of hers.

The wind began to press Elay's blouse against her breasts while she waited on her mistress patiently. She laced Ana's shoes and also bestirred herself to see that Ana's earrings were not askew. For Ana must appear every inch the dressmaker that she was. Let everyone know that she was traveling to Manila—not just to the provincial capital; and, of course, there was the old spinster aunt, too, for company—to set up a shop in the big city. It occurred to Elay that, judging from the care her mistress was taking to look well, it might well be that they were not on board a one-masted Tingloy batel with a cargo of lumber, copra, pigs, and chickens, but were still at home in the dress shop that they were leaving behind in the lumber town of Sumagi.

"How miserable I'd be without you, Elay," Ana giggled, as though somewhere she was meeting a secret lover who for certain would hold her in his arms in one wild, passionate caress.

And thinking so of her mistress made Elay more proud of her. She did not mind the dark world into which they were going. Five miles to the south was Pinamalayan town; its lights blinked faintly at her. Then along the rim of the bay, dense groves of coconuts and underbrush stood, with occasional fires marking where the few sharecroppers of the district lived. The batel had anchored at the northernmost end of the cove, and apparently five hundred yards from the boat was the palm-leaf-covered hut the old skipper of the *Ligaya* had spoken about.

"Do you see it? That's Obregano's hut." And Obregano, the old skipper explained, was a fisherman. The men who sailed up and down the eastern coast of Mindoro knew him well. There was not a seaman who lived in these parts but had gone to Obregano for food or shelter, and to this anchorage behind the northern tip of Pinamalayan Bay for the protection it offered sailing vessels against the unpredictable noroeste.

The old skipper had explained all this to Ana, and Elay had listened, little knowing that in a short while it would all be there before her. Now in the dark she saw the fisherman's hut readily. A broad shoulder of a hill rose beyond, and farther yet, the black sky looked like a silent wall.

Other women joined them on the deck to see the view for themselves. A discussion started; some members of the party did not think that it would be proper for them to spend the night in Obregano's hut. Besides the students, there were four middle-aged merchants on this voyage; since Bongabon they had plagued the women with their coarse talk and their yet coarser laughter. Although the deckhouse was the acknowledged domain of the women, the four middle-aged merchants had often slipped in and, once inside, had exchanged lewd jokes among themselves, to the embarrassment of their audience. Small wonder, Elay thought, that the prospect of spending the night in a small fisherman's hut and with those men for company did not appear attractive to the other women passengers. Her mistress Ana had made up her mind, however. She had a sense of independence that Elay admired.

Already the old aunt had joined them on deck; and Elay

said to herself, "Of course, it's for this old auntie's sake, too. She has been terribly seasick."

In the dark she saw the dinghy and silently watched it being sculled back to the batel. It drew nearer and nearer, a dark mass moving eagerly, the bow pointing in her direction. Elay heard Ana's little shrill cries of excitement. Soon two members of the crew were vying for the honor of helping her mistress safely into the dinghy.

Oh, that Ana should allow herself to be thus honored, with the seamen taking such pleasure from it all, and the old aunt, watching, pouting her lips in disapproval! "What shall I do?" Elay asked herself, anticipating that soon she herself would be the object of this chivalrous byplay. And what could the old aunt be saying now to herself? "Ah, women these days are no longer decorous. In no time they will make a virtue of being unchaste."

Elay pouted, too. And then it was her turn. She must get into that dinghy, and it so pitched and rocked. If only she could manage to have no one help her at all. But she'd fall into the water. Santa Maria! I'm safe . . .

They were off. The waves broke against the sides of the dinghy, threatening to capsize it, and continually the black depths glared at her. Her hands trembling, Elay clung tenaciously to the gunwale. Spray bathed her cheeks. A boy began to bail, for after clearing each wave the dinghy took in more water. So earnest was the boy at this chore that Elay thought the tiny boat had sprung a leak and would sink at any moment.

The sailors, one at the prow and the other busy with the oar at the stern, engaged themselves in senseless banter. Were they trying to make light of the danger? She said her prayers as the boat swung from side to side, to a rhythm set by the sailor with the oar.

Fortunately, panic did not seize her. It was the old aunt who cried "*Susmariosep!*" For with each crash of waves, the dinghy lurched precipitously. "God spare us all!" the old aunt prayed frantically.

And Ana was laughing. "Auntie! Why, Auntie, it's nothing! It's nothing at all!" For, really, they were safe. The dinghy had struck sand.

Elay's dread of the water suddenly vanished and she said to herself, "Ah, the old aunt is only making things more difficult for herself." Why, she wouldn't let the sailor with the oar lift her clear off the dinghy and carry her to the beach!

"Age before beauty," the sailor was saying to his companion. The other fellow, not to be outdone, had jumped waist-deep into the water, saying, "No, beauty above all!" Then there was Ana stepping straight, as it were, into the sailor's arms.

"Where are you?" the old aunt was calling from the shore. "Are you safe? Are you all right?"

Elay wanted to say that in so far as she was concerned she was safe, she was all right. She couldn't speak for her mistress, of course! But the seaman who had lifted the old aunt and carried her to the shore in his arms had returned. Now he stood before Elay and caught her two legs and let them rest on his forearm and then held her body up, with the other arm. Now she was clear of the dinghy, and she had to hold on to his neck. Then the sailor made three quick steps toward dry sand and then let her slide easily off his arms, and she said, "I am all right. Thank you."

Instead of saying something to her the sailor hurried away, joining the group of students that had gathered up the rise of sand. Ana's cheerful laughter rang in their midst. Then a youth's voice, clear in the wind, "Let's hurry to the fisherman's hut!"

A drizzle began to fall. Elay took a few tentative steps toward the palm-leaf hut, but her knees were unsteady. The world seemed to turn and turn, and the glowing light at the fisherman's door swung as from a boat's mast. Elay hurried as best she could after Ana and her old aunt, both of whom had already reached the hut. It was only on hearing her name that that weak, unsteady feeling in her knees disappeared.

"Elay . . ." It was her mistress, of course. Ana was standing outside the door, waiting. "My lipstick, Elay!"

An old man stood at the door of the hut. "I am Obregano, at your service," he said in welcome. "This is my home."

He spoke in a singsong that rather matched his wizened face. Pointing at a little woman pottering about the stove box at the far end of the one-room hut, he said, "And she? Well, the guardian of my home . . . in other words, my wife!"

The woman got up and welcomed them, beaming a big smile. "Feel at home. Make yourselves comfortable . . . everyone."

She helped Elay with the canvas bag, choosing a special corner for it. "It will rain harder yet tonight, but here your bag will be safe," the woman said.

The storm had come. The thatched wall shook, producing a weird skittering sound at each gust of wind. The sough of the palms in back of the hut—which was hardly the size of the deckhouse of the batel, and had the bare sand for floor—sounded like the moan of a lost child. A palm leaf that served to cover an entrance to the left of the stove box began to dance a mad, rhythmless dance. The fire in the stove leaped intermittently, rising beyond the lid of the kettle that Obregano, the old fisherman, had placed there.

And yet the hut was homelike. It was warm and clean. There was a cheerful look all over the place. Elay caught the old fisherman's smile as his wife cleared the floor of blankets, nets, and coil after coil of hempen rope, so that their guests could have more room. She sensed an affinity with her present surroundings, with the smell of the fish nets, with the dancing fire in the stove box. It was as though she had lived in this hut before. She remembered what Obregano's wife had said to her. The old woman's words were by far the kindest she had heard in a long time.

The students from Bongabon had appropriated a corner for themselves and begun to discuss supper. It appeared that a prankster had relieved one of the chicken coops of a fat pullet, and a boy asked the fisherman for permission to prepare a stew.

"I've some ginger tea in the kettle," Obregano said. "Something worth drinking in weather like this." He asked his wife for an old enameled tin cup for their guests to drink from.

As the cup was being passed around, Obregano's wife expressed profuse apologies for not preparing supper. "We have no food," she said with uncommon frankness. "We have sons, you know, two of them, both working in town. But they come home only on weekends. It is only then that we have rice."

Elay understood that, in lieu of wages, the two Obregano boys received rice. Last weekend the boys had failed to return home, however. This fact brought a sad note to Elay's new world of warm fire and familiar smells. She got out some food they had brought along from the boat—*adobo* and bread that the old aunt had put in a tin container and tucked into the canvas satchel—and offered her mistress these, going through the motions so absentmindedly that Ana chided her.

"Do offer the old man and his wife some of that, too."

Obregano shook his head. He explained that he would not think of partaking of the food—so hungry his guests must be. They needed all the food themselves, to say nothing about that which his house should offer but which in his naked poverty he could not provide. But at least they would be safe here for the night, Obregano assured them. "The wind is rising, and the rain, too. . . . Listen . . ." He pointed at the roof, which seemed to sag.

The drone of the rain set Elay's spirits aright. She began to imagine how sad and worried over her sons the old fisherman's wife must be, and how lonely—but oh how lovely!— it would be to live in this God-forsaken spot. She watched the students devour their supper, and she smiled thanks, sharing their thoughtfulness, when they offered most generously some chicken to Ana and, in sheer politeness, to the old spinster aunt also.

Yet more people from the batel arrived, and the four merchants burst into the hut discussing some problem in Bongabon municipal politics. It was as though the foul weather suited their purposes, and Elay listened with genuine interest—with compassion, even, for the small-town politicians who were being reviled and cursed.

It was Obregano who suggested that they all retire. There was hardly room for everyone, and in bringing out a rough-woven palm-leaf mat for Ana and her companions to use, Obregano picked his way in order not to step on a sprawling leg or an outstretched arm. The offer of the mat touched Elay's heart, so much so that pondering the goodness of the old fisherman and his wife took her mind away from the riddles which the students at this time were exchanging among themselves. They were funny riddles, and there was much laughter. Once she caught them throwing glances in Ana's direction.

Even the sailors who were with them on the dinghy had returned to the hut to stay and were laughing heartily at their own stories. Elay watched Obregano produce a bottle of kerosene for the lantern and then hang the lantern with a string from the center beam of the hut. She felt a new, dreamlike joy. Watching the old fisherman's wife extinguish the fire in the stove made Elay's heart throb.

Would the wind and the rain worsen? The walls of the hut shook—like a man in the throes of malarial chills. The sea kept up a wild roar, and the waves, it seemed, continually clawed at the land with strong, greedy fingers.

She wondered whether Obregano and his wife would ever sleep. The couple would be thinking: "Are our guests comfortable enough as they are?" As for herself, Elay resolved, she would stay awake. From the corner where the students slept she could hear the whine of a chronic asthma sufferer. One of the merchants snorted periodically, like a horse being plagued by a fly. A young boy, apparently dreaming, called out in a strange, frightened voice: "No, no! I can't do that! I wouldn't do that!"

She saw Obregano get up and pick his way again among the sleeping bodies to where the lantern hung. The flame was sputtering. Elay watched him adjust the wick of the lantern and give the oil container a gentle shake. Then the figure of the old fisherman began to blur and she could hardly keep her eyes open. A soothing tiredness possessed her. As she yielded easily to sleep, with Ana to her left and the old spinster aunt at the far edge of the mat to her right, the floor seemed to sink and the walls of the hut to vanish, as though the world were one vast, dark valley.

When later she awoke, she was trembling with fright. She had only a faint notion that she had screamed. What blur there had been in her consciousness before falling asleep was as nothing compared with that which followed her waking, although she was aware of much to-do and the lantern light was gone.

"Who was it?" It was reassuring to hear Obregano's voice.

"The lantern, please!" That was Ana, her voice shrill and wiry.

Elay heard, as if in reply, the crash of the sea rising in a crescendo. The blur lifted a little—"Had I fallen asleep after all? Then it must be past midnight by now." Time and place became realities again; and she saw Obregano, with a lighted matchstick in his hand. He was standing in the middle of the hut.

"What happened?"

Elay thought that it was she whom Obregano was speaking to. She was on the point of answering, although she had no idea of what to say, when Ana, sitting up on the mat beside her, blurted out, "Someone was here. Please hold up the light."

"Someone was here," Elay repeated to herself and hid her face behind Ana's shoulder. She must not let the four merchants, nor the students either, stare at her so. Caught by the lantern light, the men hardly seven steps away had turned their gazes upon her in various attitudes of amazement.

Everyone seemed eager to say something all at once. One of the students spoke in a quavering voice, declaring that he had not moved from where he lay. Another said he had been so sound asleep—"Didn't you hear me snoring?" he asked a companion, slapping him on the back—he had not even heard the shout. One of the merchants hemmed and suggested that perhaps cool minds should look into the case, carefully and without preconceived ideas. To begin with, one must know exactly what happened. He looked in Ana's direction and said, "Now, please tell us."

Elay clutched her mistress's arm. Before Ana could speak, Obregano's wife said, "This thing ought not to have happened. If only our two sons were home, they'd avenge the honor of our house." She spoke with a rare eloquence for an angry woman. "No one would then think of so base an act. Now, our good guests," she added, addressing her husband, bitterly, "why, they know you to be an aged, simple-hearted fisherman . . . nothing more. The good name of your home, of our family, is no concern of theirs."

"Evil was coming, I knew it!" said the old spinster aunt; and piping out like a bird: "Let us return to the boat! Don't be so bitter, old one," she told Obregano's wife. "We are going back to the boat."

"It was like this," Ana said, not minding her aunt. Elay lowered her head more, lest she should see those man-faces before her, loosely trapped now by the lantern's glow. Indeed, she closed her eyes, as though she were a little child afraid of the dark.

"It was like this," her mistress began again. "I was sleeping and then my maid, Elay . . ." she put an arm around Elay's shoulder. "She uttered that wild scream. I am surprised you did not hear it."

In a matter-of-fact tone, one of the merchants countered, "Suppose it was a nightmare?"

But Ana did not listen to him. "Then my maid," she continued, "this girl here . . . she's hardly twenty, mind you, and an innocent and illiterate girl, if you must all know. . . . She turned round, trembling, and clung to me . . ."

"Couldn't she possibly have shouted in her sleep?" the merchant insisted.

Obregano had held his peace all this time, but now he spoke, "Let us hear what the girl says."

And so kind were those words! How fatherly of him to have spoken so, in such a gentle and understanding way!

Elay's heart went to him. She felt she could almost run to him and, crying over his shoulder, tell him what no one, not even Ana herself, would ever know.

She turned her head a little to one side and saw that now they were all looking at her. She hugged her mistress tighter, in a childlike embrace, hiding her face as best she could.

"Tell them," Ana said, drawing herself away. "No, go on . . . speak!"

But Elay would not leave her side. She clung to her and began to cry softly.

"Nonsense!" the old aunt chided her.

"Well, she must have had a nightmare, that's all," the merchant said, chuckling. "I'm sure of it!"

At this remark Elay cried even more. "I felt a warm hand caressing my . . . my . . . my cheeks," she said, sobbing. "A warm hand, I swear," she said again, remembering how it had reached out for her in the dark, searchingly burning with a need to find some precious treasure which, she was certain of it now, she alone possessed. For how could it be that they should force her to tell them? "Someone"—the word was like a lamp in her heart—"someone wanted me," she said to herself.

She felt Ana's hand stroking her back ungently and then heard her saying, "I brought this on," then nervously fumbling about the mat. "This is all my fault. . . . My compact, please."

But Elay was inconsolable. She was sorry she could be of no help to her mistress now. She hung her head, unable to stop her tears from cleansing those cheeks that a warm hand had loved.

1950

Children of the Ash-Covered Loam

ONE DAY WHEN TARANG WAS SEVEN HIS FATHER came home from Malig with the carabao Bokal and its sled. The carabao belonged to their neighbor Longinos, who lived in the clearing across the river.

"*Harao*!" his father said, pulling Bokal to a stop.

As Tarang ran to catch the lead rope that his father had tossed over to him, Bokal flared its nostrils and gave him a good look with its big watery eyes, as if to say, "Well, Anak, here we are! Have you been good?"

He had been playing alone in the yard, in the long slack of afternoon, and had been good, except that once Nanay had said why didn't he do his playing in the hut so that at the same time he could look after his little sister Cris, who just now was learning to crawl. But that was because Nanay had wanted to stay in the shade and do her rice-pounding there, when she ought to have waited for Tatay to come and help, or for Tarang to grow up, even! So what Tarang had done was keep silence when she called. And then afterward, she was spanking Cris for not taking an afternoon nap; and Tarang heard her calling to him, "You'll see when your *tatay* comes!" And so he walked to the riverbank and gathered some guavas, eating the ripe ones as fast as he got them, and now he was belching, his breath smelling of guava. Perhaps his hair, too, smelled of guava, for why should Bokal flare its nostrils that way?

With Cris astride her hip, Nanay came down from the hut, saying, "You might give that hard-headed son of yours a thrashing for staying in the sunshine all afternoon."

15

But Tatay only laughed. "Really!" he said, and then he asked, "Would you like to know what I've brought here?"

"What is it this time?" Nanay asked.

There was a basket on the sled that had been hitched to Bokal, and Tarang looked to see what it contained.

"If you must know, it's a pig!" Tatay said, and led the carabao away to the *hinagdong* tree.

"Now don't you try touching it yet," his mother warned Tarang.

"It's so that the boy will have something to look after," Tatay was saying from under the tree across the yard, where he had tethered the carabao.

Tarang tugged at the basket that lay on the floor of the sled, and, indeed, two black feet presently thrust out of a hole in one corner, and from another sprang the third. Tatay cut the basket open with his bolo, and the pig struggled out. "It's for you to look after," he told the boy.

Nanay was standing there beside him and, having swung Cris over to her other hip, began scratching the belly of the pig with her big toe.

"Do this often and it will become tame," she said. And to Tatay, "Now, if you hold Cris a while . . ."

Then she took the bolo and, crossing the yard, she went past the hinagdong tree where Bokal was and disappeared in the underbrush. She returned with six freshly ripe papayas; then and there she wanted to cut them up to feed to the pig, but Tatay said, "Here, you hold Cris yourself . . ."

He got back his bolo from Nanay, slipped it into its sheath, and hurried down the path to the *kaingin*. Tarang could see the tall, dead trees of the clearing beyond the hinagdong and the second growth. The afternoon sun made the bark of the trees glisten like the bolo blade itself.

He thought his father would be away very long, but Tatay

was back soon with a length of tree trunk which had not been completely burned that day they set fire to the clearing. The fire had devoured only the hollow of the trunk; what Tatay had brought was, in fact, a trough that the kaingin had made for them. Now Tatay trimmed the ends neatly and flattened one side so that the trough would sit firm on the ground.

They all sat there watching the pig eating from the trough. In a short while its snout was black from rubbing against the burned bottom and sides.

"Where did the pig come from? You have not said one word," Nanay said.

"Well, there I was in the barrio. And whom do I see but Paula . . . when all the time I meant not to get even a shadow of her."

Tarang stared at both of them, not knowing what they were talking about. Cris sat on Nanay's arm, watching the pig also, and making little bubbling sounds in her mouth.

"We shall pay everything we owe them next harvest," Nanay said.

"Well, there I was and she saw me," Tatay went on. "She asked could I go to her house and have my noon meal there? So I went and ate in the kitchen. Then she asked could I fetch some water and fill the jars? And could I split some firewood? And could I go out there in the corner of her yard and have a look at her pigs?

"She had three of them, one a boar," Tatay went on. "And if I wasn't afraid really that I'd be told to fix the fence or the pen, I am a liar this very minute."

"But for a *ganta* or five *chupas* of salt, maybe. Why not?" Nanay asked.

"You guessed right. She said, 'Fix it, for the ganta of salt that you got from the store last time.' "

"Well, there you are!"

"That's the trouble, there I was. But she said: 'For your little boy to look after, if you like. Yes, why not take home one sow with you?' And I said: 'For my boy?' Because, believe me, I was proud and happy Paula remembered our *anak*. She said, 'If you can fatten it, let it have a litter, then all the better for all of us.' So I've brought home the pig."

Nanay tossed more portions of ripe papaya into the trough. Tarang scratched the pig's back gently as it continued to eat, making loud noises, not only with its mouth but also with something else inside its belly.

"If there is a litter, we are to have half," his father was saying; and then his mother said:

"That is good enough."

"Well, then, feed it well, Anak!" his father said.

"And you said there was a boar in that pen?" his mother asked.

"A big and vigorous boar," his father said.

Nanay smiled and then walked over to the kitchen to start a fire in the stove. When the pig had devoured all the ripe papayas, Tatay got a rope and made a harness of it around the pig's shoulder.

"Here, better get it used to you," Tatay said.

So Tarang dragged the pig across the yard. His father led the way through the bush, to the edge of the kaingin nearest the hut. There they tied the pig to a tree stump. Then his father cut some stakes with which to make a pen.

They did not make a full-fledged pen, only one with two sides. For already they had the two other sides right there: the outcropping roots of the old *dao* tree were like walls meant for their pen. The rest was easy. Tarang shoved the pig into the enclosure and then his father went back to the hut to fetch the trough.

He fed the pig with ripe papayas as well as green, and the

good thing was that Tatay did not get cross with him over the bolo, which he was not usually encouraged to use. Now he simply strapped it to his waist and headed straight for the bush.

He brought back *ubod* from the sugar palm; its soft portions Nanay would save up for supper; the rest she'd allow him to take down to the pig.

There was the rice husk, too. Before, it did not matter whether Nanay saved the chaff, once the rice was pounded; from the mortar she would collect the rice in her wide, flat winnowing basket and, with the wind helping her, clean the grains right there under the hinagdong tree at the edge of the yard. Now it would no longer do to leave the rice husk there on the ground. The kitchen-wash mixed with rice husk won much favor with the sow; and for ever so long after feeding-time, there would be the brown band of rice husk around its mouth.

One day Nanay came home from the kaingin with welts across her cheek and over the valley of her nose. Had someone struck her with a whip? But Tatay did not seem worried. He laughed at her, in fact, and Nanay had to say something.

"I only went to the thicket for some rattan with which to fix the pen."

"Now which pen?" Tatay asked.

"The sow's."

Tatay said: "You could have waited; that was work for us."

"Still, work that had to be done," Nanay said. "And but for the swelling of the sow's belly, what do you think could have happened?"

"We did allow for the swelling of that belly," Tatay said.

"Still, I had to get the rattan," Nanay said.

"And you hurt your face," Tatay said, touching the scratches gently.

Tarang also touched the valley of her nose. She continued: "I stepped on a twig. A vine sprang from nowhere and struck me."

Tatay laughed over that one heartily. "It was as though you had stolen something, and then somebody had gone after you and caught you!"

"Next time, I'll leave the pen alone," Nanay said.

But during the days that followed they were all too busy with work in the kaingins to bother with anything else, really. In the nearby clearings, people had started planting; and so that later on they would come over to help, Tatay and Nanay offered their work in advance. They were often away out there, leaving Tarang alone in the hut, alone to cook his own meals and fetch water from the well near the riverbank. It would be hardly midafternoon, but already he would start out for the underbrush in search of ubod or ripe papayas; and before the sun had dropped behind the forest, he had fed his sow.

He was walking down the path from the kaingin one afternoon when he saw Tia Orang in the hut. He had seen her many times before, on days when Nanay and Tatay took him to the barrio, and he was not a little frightened of her then. The old midwife wore a hempen skirt dyed the color of tan bark, which is like brown clay; and so were her blouse and kerchief.

"And where would they be?" she asked the boy.

"Across the river."

"Where exactly? I have come for the planting."

"In the clearing of Mang Longinos, perhaps," the boy said. "We are not yet planting."

"Now be good enough to give me a drink of water, Anak," the old midwife said. "Then I shall be on my way."

She reached for the dipper of water that he brought her.

She drank, and then, putting down the dipper, tweaked Tarang on the leg. "If I do not see your mother, Anak, tell her that Tia Orang has come. Tell of my passing through, and of my helping in the planting when the time comes."

For a long time afterward Tarang remembered how they spent morning after morning in the kaingin, gathering pieces of burned wood and piling them up and then burning them again. Some pieces were too heavy to lift, even with all three—Nanay, Tatay, and himself—helping together; other pieces were light enough, and he would take them to the edge of the clearing, where his father laid out a fence by piling the wood between freshly cut staves and keeping these in place with rattan.

It was a pity to have Cris left behind in the hut, tied to the middle of the floor, lest she should crawl over to the steps, down the dirt of the kitchen, past the stove box, then over to the threshold, and finally out to the yard; often they returned to the hut to find her asleep, some portion of string wound tight round her legs.

But, one morning, instead of leaving Cris behind, Nanay took her to the kaingin. That was the day Tatay left the hut very early and returned with a white pullet under her arm, and then he and Nanay had a quarrel.

"You found the chicken in the riverbed? Is that what you might say?" she demanded.

"I came from Longinos's place, if you must know."

"And the pullet?"

"Look in your hamper," Tatay said.

Nanay pulled out the hamper from the corner and, in the half-light from the window, opened it and looked through her clothes one by one.

"The *camisa* that Paula gave me . . . it's gone," she said, almost in tears.

"A camisa seven years too worn out, what does it matter now?" Tatay laughed at her.

"So you bartered it for a pullet . . . for that *dumalaga*?" Nanay said.

"It will bring us luck, have no regrets," Tatay said.

They followed him to the kaingin, but when they reached the edge, where the fence was waist-high, Tatay asked Tarang's mother to stay behind. They left her and Cris sitting on a log. Tarang followed Tatay past the *dao* tree where the pigpen was, and the smell of the trough followed him to the middle of the kaingin.

They stopped near a tree stump that was knee-high and motioned to him to get no closer, for now he was holding the dumalaga with one hand, letting its wings flap like pieces of rag in the breeze, and he had pulled out his bolo. No, Tarang couldn't get any closer. Tatay laid the pullet's neck upon the flat of the tree stump and, without a word, severed its head. Was that a red streak that cut an arc toward the ash-covered ground? Tatay held the headless pullet up with one hand, to let the blood spurt well and make a long leap.

"Go, Evil Spirits of the land! Go, now!" Tatay was saying. "This land is ours now! We shall make it yield rich crops!"

Tarang looked back in the direction where Nanay and Cris sat waiting, and at first he did not see them. Beyond the clearing's edge loomed the half-dark of the forest, and a cloud had covered the rising sun and changed the morning to early evening.

Tatay had put his bolo back into its sheath and was calling for Nanay and Cris to come.

"Then do we start planting now?" Nanay asked.

"You three wait here, while I get the seed," Tatay said and walked down the trail to the hut.

He returned with Tio Longinos and Tia Pulin and Tio

Adang, and they were all of them provided with short wooden sticks sharpened at the ends for making holes in the ground. Tarang made one of his own. But he was poor at it; he was as slow as Nanay, who could hardly bend from having to have Cris astride her hip. After a while his stick got blunted. Tatay, handing him the bolo, said he should sharpen it again. Tarang's hand began to tremble. Cold sweat gathered on his brow, and the ash-covered ground seemed raw with the smell of the chicken's blood.

"You and Cris," Tatay said, taking the bolo from him. "You stay in the shade and let your mother work."

And so they looked about the edge of the clearing for the *buri* palm that had the best shade. Nanay cut some leaves and spread them on the ground. There she seated Cris and said to Tarang, "Keep your sister from crying, at least."

But, of course, he could do nothing to stop her, and Cris cried herself hoarse. She would not let him hold her; they chased each other round and round, even beyond the boundary of the leaves. It hurt his knees crawling. What stopped her finally was the sound that the wind made as it passed through and over the palm leaves, for it was a strange sound, like that of drums far away.

Toward noon, Tatay called everyone together. They gathered in the hot sun near the tree stump where the dumalaga had been killed. Already Tio Longinos and Tia Pulin and Tia Adang were gathered there when Nanay, who had gone to pick up Cris, reached the tree stump.

"Keep out of the way, Anak," Tatay said, for Longinos was setting up a small cross made of *banban* reeds.

He stepped back, but not so far away as not to hear. Longinos was now talking to the cross.

"Let citronella grass give fragrance," he was saying, pulling a sheaf of the lemon grass from the pouch at his waist, where he kept his betel nut and chewing things. "Let ginger appease the Evil Ones. Let iron give weight to the heads of rice on this clearing."

Tarang edged closer. Using his father's arm, which was akimbo, as a window to peep from, he now saw the bits of ginger and the three two-inch nails that Longinos had placed at the foot of the reed cross.

"It is now too hot to work, isn't it," Longinos said, grinning away his tiredness. His face glistened with sweat, and he led the way, making a new path across the ash-covered ground.

Tarang brought up the rear, and he saw many holes that the sticks had made. They had not been properly covered. He stopped and tapped the seed grains gently in with his big toe. He wandered around in this way, eyes lowered and quick to catch the yellow husk of grains, for they were like bits of gold on the ashy ground. He would stop and press each little mound of grain gently, now with his left big toe, now with his right. Shorter and shorter his shadow grew until it was no more than a blot on the ground, moving as deftly as he moved among the tree stumps and over the burned-out logs.

He heard much talking back and forth afterwards about how Tatay had planted the clearing a little too soon, that Tia Orang ought to have come, that they might have waited for her, Nanay said. But what was done was done, Tatay argued.

That afternoon they visited the kaingin, Tarang joining Nanay and Tatay there after he had brought the feed for the sow. It seemed to him that the ground was so dry, it could well be that he was walking on sand. Nanay feared that ants would soon make off with the grain.

That evening they sat outside in the yard and watched the sky. There were no stars. A black night covered the world. Somewhere to the west, beyond the mountain range, rain had come. Twice lightning tore at the darkness, as though a torch were being used to burn some dry underbrush in a kaingin up there in the clouds.

They had to have an early supper because Nanay said that, if a storm should come, it would be difficult to do any cooking. The roof over their stove could leak. The heat that they had been having these months had perhaps turned the buri shingles to shreds.

They went to bed early, too.

"There, what's done is done!" Tatay said, and sat on the mat, cocking his ears.

For it was rain. Tarang thought he might watch it, only it was rather late in the night. He was tired and sleepy still.

Tatay, of course, had rushed to the window, hoping perhaps to see the rain shoot arrows across the yard.

Now, Tarang could hardly keep himself from getting up also. He had made it as far as the window when his mother awoke and called him sternly back to bed. He had to content himself with listening to the rain on the roof.

It proved a brief rainburst only. Before daybreak it was all over.

"There is work for us to do, don't you know?" Tatay said after breakfast, knotting his bolo string round his waist. "The pig . . . your sow, understand? With the rains now coming . . ."

Tarang understood readily that they must raise a roof over the pen. He set out eagerly, doing everything that his father bade him. He gathered the buri leaves required and took them to the foot of the dao tree. While Tatay disappeared in the bush to get some vines for tying the leaves onto the makeshift beams, Tarang struggled with his leaves, dragging the fronds one by one, the noise this made like that of a snake running through a *kogon* field.

They were not quite through with the roof when the sky darkened again. From afar thunder rumbled, only the storm seemed rather close this time.

It was a long, dreary-looking afternoon. It was warm, but he knew that soon it would be raining very hard, perhaps as hard as he had ever seen rain fall before. When he set out to gather ripe papayas for the sow, it was already drizzling.

Nanay had made him promise not to stay away too long, and now he came running to the hut. The thunderstorm was right behind him. Panting, he strode into the kitchen, unknotting the string of his father's bolo from his waist.

"Mind to look for mushrooms tomorrow," Tatay was saying.

Why? Do mushrooms come with thunderstorms? Tarang wondered. All through supper he asked about mushrooms, and now it seemed that with each flash of lightning the million and one of them that grow wild the whole world over pushed their spongy little umbrellas an inch or so toward the sky.

The drizzle was heavier now, and an owl kept hooting somewhere beyond the bamboo brakes across the river. Then the calls stopped. Tarang and his father sat there before the stove box watching Nanay, who was starting to cook rice for supper. Already the real rain was here.

There was the sound of shuffling feet in the yard, and when Nanay looked through the open door, she said, "Why, it is Tia Orang!"

The old woman dropped the frond of buri that she had used for an umbrella in the rain and clambered up the hut. Nanay called out to Tatay, who had gone to the pigpen to see that the roof they had fixed over it was secure enough and would not be blown away, should strong winds come along with the rain, as they often did.

"The midwife is here," Nanay called. And to Tia Orang, "Now you must stay the night with us."

The other said, "Then, how goes life with you?"

"The same."

"Don't I see a change? Don't I see life growing with you?"

Tarang sat there by the stove fire, idly tending the pot of vegetable stew for supper.

Nanay was saying, "There's nothing in me to be seen!" And, passing her hand up and down her belly, "Look, nothing at all! Nothing yet!"

"Cris is hardly two, that's why? But—" the old one became a little excited—"but time enough, time enough! And when it's time, I will surely remember to come," Tia Orang said.

Tatay appeared at the door with a buri umbrella of his own. He greeted Tia Orang with much show of respect.

"To be sure," he said, "let her stay the night with us," he told Nanay. "Now is supper ready?" He turned to Tarang, asking, "Anak, is supper ready?"

So Nanay came down, leaving Cris upstairs with Tia Orang, and helped get the supper ready. She removed the pot of vegetable stew from the fire and started pouring some of it into the bowls. There were not enough bowls for all five of them, Cris included, and Nanay said Tarang could use for his bowl the coconut-shell dipper for the drinking water.

"But," Tia Orang asked, laughing, "should I not first of all earn my supper, no?"

Nanay had almost everything ready—the rice, and then a little pinch of salt on a banana leaf, and the bowls of stew, all of them on the bamboo floor.

"If you want to," Nanay said. "Do I spread the mat?"

"If you want to," Tia Orang said.

"It's bound to come; it's bound to come!" Tia Orang said,

kneeling on the mat, one hand pressing Nanay's abdomen. She beckoned to Tatay, "Be of help!"

It was as if Tatay had been waiting all this time. He was ready with a coconut shell containing bits of crushed ginger roots soaked in oil. Tia Orang dipped her fingers into the mess, then rubbed her palms together and commenced kneading the muscles of Nanay's belly. The smell of ginger root and coconut oil made Tarang sneeze. The shell with the medicine Tarang remembered from the many occasions Nanay appeared to be ill, and the kneading was just about as familiar. Tatay did exactly the same whenever anyone of them had pains in the stomach.

Tatay had lighted the *lamparilla* and set it on the floor, upon an empty sardine can. In the light, which was yellow like the back part of a leaf just starting to become dry, Tia Orang's face looked as though made of earth.

Nanay was smiling at her. She lay smiling at everyone, her eyes traveling from one face to the next. A blush reddened her cheeks.

Tia Orang and Nanay talked, but mostly in whispers. Tarang caught only a few words. Then, aloud, the old woman called to Tatay, and Nanay got up and rolled up the mat. She let it rustle softly.

"Let us have supper now, no?" Tatay asked.

Wind from the open doorway fanned the wood in the stove, and, because this was bright enough, Tatay blew the lamparilla out.

They sat around the plate of rice that Nanay had set earlier on the floor. Tarang felt his hunger grow with each mouthful of rice, and he ate heartily, sipping the broth of the vegetable stew, then mixing the rice with the tomatoes and the sweet-potato leaves and the dried anchovies, gray and headless, in his coconut-shell bowl.

Tia Orang talked a great deal. Perhaps to conceal her appetite, Tarang thought. She talked about the old days in Malig, those days when people did not go so far inland as Loob-Loob but stayed most of the time in the barrio or else went only as far as Bakawan. Tarang listened because she spoke of Evil Ones and of Spirits, and he remembered the kaingin and Longinos and the citronella and the nails and the ginger root.

"Now, there was that man who lost his arm felling a tree, Tia Orang was saying, "and another who, for forgetting his reed cross and all those things of the *gapi,* began to suffer a strange sickness."

Tarang cocked his ears.

"It was pus that he began to pass instead of water, let me tell you. Do you know what happened to his wife as well? The woman was with child, and when she was about to deliver, the misfortune came. No child came forth, but when the labor was done, there were leeches and nothing else! Fat and blood-red, and they filled a whole wooden bowl."

Nanay stopped eating suddenly. She reached out for drinking water, which was in a coconut shell laid there also upon the floor. Tatay ate in silence, leaving nothing in his bowl. He looked up at Tia Orang as if to ask, "Now, what else?"

Outside it was as though someone with a brightly burning torch were driving bees off a hive up there in the sky. Beyond the western mountains was another early evening thunderstorm.

At the corner where Nanay was spreading a sleeping mat for Tia Orang, the wind brushed the siding of buri leaves. "Mind to gather those mushrooms tomorrow, just as I've said," Tatay kept telling her.

They went to bed very early. Tarang thought he should stay in one corner, far from Nanay. He was a man now, he felt.

He took an empty buri sack, the one for keeping *palay* in, and pressed it flat with his feet. It made a nice bed on the floor, there against the wall, near the doorstep.

On her mat Tia Orang stirred wakefully, but she could be heard snoring. Many times Tarang awoke, the strange noises in the old woman's nose and mouth frightening him not a little. It was as if she were uttering strange words to strangers, to people who did not belong to the world of men and women. Tarang strained his ears, but he could not catch even one word. Yet there was no doubt that she was talking to someone even now in her sleep. She stirred and turned to the wall, and now she was talking to the buri leaves with which the wall was made.

The thunderstorm came closer. For the first time since he could remember, the rain poured with loud thuds on the roof. It must be falling all over the forest too, he thought, all over the empty river and as far down as the swamps that surrounded the barrio of Malig by the sea.

In his mind, half-awake, Tarang thought the rain was making music now, shaking songs off the swaying treetops on the fringe of the kaingin. Then he heard Tatay get up from bed. Perhaps Tatay, too, had heard the music of the rain, only Tatay was hurrying down the hut, knotting his bolo string round his waist as he slipped past the door.

Tarang thought he could hear something else besides— the sow in the pen, under the dao tree. He listened more carefully. He could hear the grunting. There were little noises, too. A squirming litter, protesting against the cold. Surely, with wet snouts tugging at its teats, a sow could be annoyed. The belly would be soft like a rag.

"That's something to see!" He got up quietly and slipped out the door into the rain.

It seemed that at this very hour the rice grains, too, would be pressing forward, up the ash-covered loam, thrusting forth their tender stalks through the sodden dirt. He thought he caught the sound that the seeds also made.

The ground was not too wet. In his haste, Tarang struck a tree stump with his big toe; and the hurt was not half as keen as it might have been, not half as sharp as his hunger for knowing, for seeing with his own eyes how life emerged from this dark womb of the land at this time of night.

1951

The Morning Star

THE SAILOR WENT BACK TO THE OUTRIGGERED
boat and returned with a lantern. It lighted up the footpath
before him and also his flat, unshod feet. He walked in a
slow, shuffling manner, the lantern in his hand swinging in
rhythm.

"Can't you walk faster?" the old man shouted from the
coconut grove.

Instead of saying something in reply, the sailor shuffled
on, neither hastening nor slowing his gait.

"You're a turtle, that's what," said the old man.

As the sailor approached, the lantern caught the entrance
of the makeshift shelter. Then the oval of light completely
engulfed the shelter, which was shaped like a pup tent and
built of coconut leaves woven into loose shingles. A matting
of coconut leaves was spread on the ground and, walking
across it, the old man hung the lantern from a ridgepole at
the far end. A woman sat in one corner, her back half-turned
to the entrance.

"Now, if you aren't stupid! Quite like a turtle, really," the
old man said to the sailor.

"Ha?" the other said, with a twang.

The old man had expected that; there was something
wrong with the sailor's tongue. "And how about the jute
sacks and the blankets?" the old man said. "Didn't I tell you
to get them?"

"Ha?" came the sailor's reply.

"Stop it!" said the old man, angrily. "If you weren't born
that way, I'd give you a thrashing." He waved him away. "Be
off! And while you're at it, bring over some water. There's no

saying whether we'll find drinking water hereabouts. Would you care for supper, Marta?"

"No, thank you," said the woman in the hut.

"It'll be best to get some food ready, though," said the old man. "We've salmon in the boat."

The sailor had shuffled away, the coconut fronds on the ground rustling softly as he stepped on them.

"Bring over a tin of salmon. And also the pot of rice we have on the stove box," the old man called after the sailor.

From somewhere a bird uttered a shrill cry; and the old man spoke to the woman again. "If you'll step out of there just a while, Marta . . ."

"I am quite comfortable here, Uncle," she said.

"But you should be walking about, instead of sitting down like that."

"It seems better here," said the woman. But later she said, "All right."

"I'll build a fire," the old man said.

The bird's call came again, in a note of wild urgency. "That's the witch bird. I can tell for certain," the woman said. "It takes the newborn away."

"No, it's not the witch bird," the old man said.

He gathered some dry leaves and twigs and in a minute had a fire blazing.

"Still, it's a fine time for having a baby, Uncle. Isn't it?"

"It's God's will," the old man said. Marta was laughing at herself. "We'll do the best we can. Walk about; stretch your legs; hold on to a coconut trunk over there, if it hurts you so."

"I'm quite all right, Uncle," said Marta.

The fire crackled, and the old man added more leaves and twigs. The blaze illuminated the large boles of the coconut palms.

33

The clear sky peered through the fronds of the palms, but there were no stars. The night had a taut, timorous silence, disturbed only by the crackling of the fire.

The woman walked up and down, not venturing beyond the space lighted up by the fire. She was a squat, well-built woman. Her arms and legs were full-muscled, like those of a man. Her distended belly and large breasts would not have made any difference.

The old man watched her with unending curiosity. Like him, she wore a field jacket, the sleeves rolled up, being too long. Her skirt was of a thick olive-drab material, made from fatigues that some American soldier had discarded.

"Is that his name printed on there?" the old man asked.

In the firelight the letters "Theodore C. Howard" could be read in white stenciling on the back of the drab green jacket.

"Oh no, Uncle," said Marta. "This isn't his. He gave me three woolen blankets, though."

"That's fair," said the old man.

"What do you mean, Uncle? Please don't tease me," said Marta.

"Well, others do get more than that. For their labor, I mean. You worked as a laundrywoman, I suppose."

"Yes, Uncle," Marta replied. "But afterwards, we lived together—three weeks. We had a hut near Upper Mangyan. You could see the whole camp of the Army from there." With her hands, she held on to her belt, a rattan string, as she spoke. "It pains so, at times. Well, I washed clothes for a living, Uncle. That's what I went there for."

"Did you earn any money?"

"No, Uncle. I'm never for making money. He said one day, 'Here are twenty pesos,' " she said with a laugh. "He had a way of talking to me and never saying my name, as though I had no name. The others, the ones I only washed clothes for, had a nickname for me. 'Sweet Plum,' I remember. That's how they called me—'Sweet Plum.' What's a plum, Uncle? They say it's a fruit."

"I don't know," said the old man. "In our country, we have no such fruit."

"He would not call me 'Sweet Plum,' even. And, as I said, he wanted to give me the money. 'What for?' I said. And he said, 'For your mother.' But I have no mother, I told him so. 'Well, for your father and brothers and sisters.' But I have no such folk. I told him so. I said, 'Keep your money. I love you, so keep your money.' And he was angry, and he swore and then left the hut. I never saw him again, but he left me three woolen blankets."

The old man listened to the story with great interest, but now that it was over, he made no comment beyond getting up and thoughtfully tending the fire.

"No, Uncle. You're wrong to think I ever earned money," Marta said. She walked a few paces and returned to the fire-side. "By the way, Uncle, how much does it cost to go to San Paulino in your boat?"

"That's where you live?"

She nodded her head.

"For you, nothing. Not a centavo."

"I can give you one of my woolen blankets."

"The trip will cost you nothing."

"Of course, you'll say, 'What a foolish woman she is! To think that she does not know when her time comes!' But truly, Uncle, the days are the same to me. The nights are the same. I can't count days and months. Maybe, Uncle, I'll never grow old. Do you think I'll never grow old?"

The old man did not know what to say. A soft chuckle, and that was all.

"And I am going home. Am I not foolish, Uncle?"

To humor her, the old man said, "Yes, you are quite fool-ish. A good thing you found my boat, no?"

"I feel lucky, yes," Marta said. "I must leave, that was all. Maybe, it isn't my time yet. The long walk from Upper Mangyan, and then three days on the beach, before finding your boat. . . . Maybe, this is only the seventh month. How long is nine months, Uncle?"

The old man wished he could give a good answer. "Nine months," he said finally.

"I understand. You old men know a lot. Now, don't laugh, Uncle. I've been married before, and this man I married was an old man, too. May he rest in peace. Oh, it pains so! Here, right here!" She indicated the approximate location of the pain.

"Walking relieves it, so they say."

The leaves crackled softly on the ground as she trod upon them with her bare foot. She went back and forth, and talked on as if to amuse herself.

"Now, this man was a tailor. You see, I worked as a servant in a rich man's house. And this tailor said, one day, 'You don't have to work so hard like that, Marta. Come live with me.' Ah, you men are tricky. Aren't you, Uncle?"

"Sometimes," the old man couldn't help saying. "Some men are, I must say," he agreed readily.

"This tailor, he saw how industrious I was . . . and, I dare say, I am. Because God made me so; with the build of an animal, how can one be lazy? There's not a kind of work you men can do that I can't do also. That's a woman for you! My tailor was pleased with me. I was a woman and a man all in one, and he was so happy he stopped becoming a tailor and took instead to visiting with neighbors, talking politics and things like that." She stopped short, and then as if suddenly remembering something, she said: "But he left me no child. Oh, he fooled me so, Uncle!"

"Well, you'll have one soon, I must say," said the old man.

"As I was saying, I lived with this old tailor. He was a widower and had been lonely, and now he was kind to me. But he died of consumption . . . he had it for a long time . . . the year the war started. I went back to the rich man's house where I had worked before. When the Americans came back I said to this rich man, 'I am going away. Only for a short time, though. I hear they pay well at the camp of the Army, if you can wash clothes and do things like that. When I have enough money, I'll come back.' That's what I said. Oh, oh! It hurts so!"

"It's time the sailor returns," said the old man. "Does it pain much?"

"Ah, but pain never bothers me, Uncle. Didn't I tell you I am built like an animal? This tailor, he used to beat me. I didn't care. I can stand anything, you know. I chopped wood and pounded rice for him. I was quite sorry when he died. That's the truth, Uncle."

She stopped and laughed, amused more than ever perhaps at the way she had been talking. The old man looked at her quizzically.

"And you'll bring this baby home to San Paulino?" he said.

"Why, of course, Uncle. It'll be so tiny, so helpless . . . you know. Why do you ask?"

The old man hesitated, but in the end he decided to tell her: "There are places . . . in the city, for example . . . where they'll take care of babies like that . . ."

"But can they take care of him better than I? That's impossible, Uncle," the woman said, excitedly. "Oh, it hurts so! . . I do like . . . oh! . . to look after him myself . . ."

37

The firelight caught her faint smile. She had a common-looking face, but her eyes were pretty and big and smiling.

She had stopped talking. The sailor appeared in their midst, saying "Ha!"

"Warm the salmon in the fire," said the old man.

He took the jute sacks and the blankets into the shelter and prepared a bed. Outside, in the light of the fire, the sailor opened the salmon can with his bolo and began drinking the soup in the can.

"Can't you wait for me?"

The old man crawled out of the hut, annoyed partly because the sailor had begun to eat and partly because Marta was groaning.

"Don't wail there like a sow," he told her gruffly.

Then he sat before the pot of rice that the sailor brought over.

The old man said nothing in reply. He and the sailor ate hurriedly, making noises with their mouths.

"Ha!" said the sailor, in that helpless way of his, looking in Marta's direction.

"She doesn't care for food. She said so," the old man explained. And to Marta, he said, "If it's too much to bear, you may go in. We'll keep some of the salmon for you. Afterwards, you'll be so hungry."

Marta followed his advice, crawling into the hut. Her head struck the lantern that hung from the ridgepole, and for a while the lantern swung about, the oval of light dancing on the ground.

"I'll be with you in a minute," said the old man. "Why you've to let me do this, I don't know." It seemed he had become a different person from the *uncle* Marta knew a while ago; he felt the change in himself.

"Uncle," the woman called from in the shelter, "what's a man called when he does a midwife's business?"

The old man was washing his mouth with water from the container the sailor had brought from their outriggered boat. When he was through, he said: "You horrible creature! I'm now sure of it! You've fooled me. You planned all this. . . . You're more clever than I thought."

There was silence in the shelter. From afar the night bird called again, clearly and hauntingly. The sailor, calling the old man's attention to the bird, said, "Ha, ha!" He pointed with his finger at the darkness, but the old man did not mind him.

The silence grew tense, although there were soft noises from the shelter, noises that the movement of feet and arms and body made upon the matting, as if a sow were indeed lying there to deliver a litter. The lantern glow fell full upon the woman's upraised knees. She had covered them with a blanket.

"Uncle!" she called frantically.

Before going in the old man looked up at the sky. There was a lone star at last, up in the heavens. He could see it through the palm fronds. He'd like to remember that. He wished he could see a moon, too, and that he knew for certain how high the tide was at the beach; for, later, he'd recall all this. But there were no other signs. There was only this star.

"I'm so frightened, Uncle," Marta was saying, her voice hoarse and trembling. "And it hurts so! Uncle, it will be the death of me!"

"Stop this foolish talk," said the old man angrily. "Pray to God. He is kind," he said.

His hands and knees were shaking. He knelt beside Marta, ready to be of assistance.

"Oh . . . oh . . . oh! Uncle, I want to die, I want to die!" she cried, clutching his hand.

When the sailor heard the squall of the child he said "Ha! Ha!" with joy. He wanted to see the child, but the old man told him to go away.

"Go!" the old man said, waving his arms.

The sailor returned to his sleeping place and lay as before. The night was warm and restful, and soon he was fast asleep.

The old man joined him under the coconut tree, their feet touching and pointing toward the smouldering fire. Through the palm fronds the old man could see the sky growing light, for soon it would be morning. The star peered at him as before through the thick coconut palm leaves. It had watched over them all this time.

The old man turned and, using his arm for a pillow, tried to sleep. The sailor was snoring peacefully. The old man could see Marta in the shelter, her legs flat on the mat and the child in a bundle beside her.

The old man fell asleep thinking of the child, for it was a boy. A gust of wind woke him up, and when he opened his eyes he did not realize at first where he was. He felt glad he had been of help to the woman, and he wondered if in any way he had been unkind to her. He wished he had not called her a sow and had been gentle with her. He sat up and saw the lantern in the shelter.

"Are you all right?" he called, for he heard the woman stir.

She did not answer but sat up, moving in a slow, deliberate way, her shadow covering the child like a blanket.

"It's the witch bird, Uncle," she said in a tired, faraway voice. "Did you hear the witch bird? Now he is dead. . . . Uncle, he is dead!"

The old man lowered the lantern. It had a faint blue flame.

The baby beside her was limp and gray, like the blanket wrapped around it.

"You're a sow, that's what you are! God Almighty," he crossed himself, "may You have mercy on us!"

"Believe me, Uncle. . . . It's the witch bird."

The sailor had wakened. He got up and sat, hugging his knees, and stared at the old man.

"You build a fire, turtle!" the old man shouted at him. "Don't you see it's so dark?"

"Ha!" the sailor said.

1950

The Blue Skull
and the Dark Palms

AS SHE STOOD BEFORE HER CLASS, MISS INOCEN-
cio, the substitute teacher, caught a glimpse of him. The
roan stallion neighed as though it had sighted a mare in the
barrio street. The next moment thick chalk-white dust rose
in the air, settling long after horse and rider had disappeared
into the heart of the village.

She knew then that in an hour or so the school inspector
would come for a visit. She stared at the clock atop the empty
bookcase that stood against the thatched wall; it was four
o'clock. Leaving her desk, she walked to the window. The
afternoon sun reached out toward it, pouring into the room a
warm gush of July sunshine.

Then Miss Inocencio did something strange: she looked
furtively at the garden outside, that patch of shrubbery and
grass where her pupils hoped to plant hibiscus and roses,
spanish flags and sunflowers; where the old well stood, its
depths long since unplumbed, its water unused. She regarded
the abandoned garden as though someone stood there—a
man, perhaps her lover—when of course there was no one
to be seen; no one to share secrets with, unless this be the
blocks of stone that rimmed the well and which now in her
mind's ear seemed to say: "True, there's been a war. But we
are ready . . . aren't we? . . . to start all over again."

Did the children hear the voice? They looked up at her
from behind their desks, and she dropped the pencil in her
hand. "You know your respective assignments?" she asked
her wards, and several voices answered in a respectful chorus:

"Yes, Ma'am."

"And remember," she addressed the boys in particular as she bent to pick up her pencil, "we must work on the garden today."

This was received with eagerness, and she desisted from telling the class about the school inspector. Already the boys were leaving their seats with much stamping and scraping of feet, re-creating the excitement of last week when the old school garden had presented itself as their common concern. "But we shall bring over our hoes and shovels, Ma'am!" . . . "And we've seeds, Ma'am; several packages that an American soldier gave us." . . . "We shall fix the well, too. We shall need water for the flowers!" . . . "Mind then, not to touch the water now," Miss Inocencio had said. "It's much too dirty to drink from . . . that well out there," she had warned them; and from the corner of her eye she had watched her favorite, Leoncio, looking at her lips closely as he allowed this modest adjuration to sink into his soul.

Now it was the favored Leoncio who said the first "Good afternoon, sir," when with flared and quivering nostrils the school inspector, tall and erect, stood there at the door. He had come earlier than she had expected. The children said their greeting, not too shyly; the visitor smiled in turn and complimented Miss Inocencio on her pupils' performance.

"Thank you, sir." she said, blushing. Leoncio, walking respectfully past the visitor, led the boys out to the porch. "It's their Gardening Period, sir," Miss Inocencio explained. "Perhaps you'd like to step in, sir?"

As the visitor crossed the threshold, the sunlight from the window fell upon his cuffless trousers. "Are the textbooks coming, sir?" Miss Inocencio asked eagerly.

"In a week or so," the visitor replied, looking around the room.

"And the new blackboards, too?"

Miss Inocencio was given the assurance that both the books and the blackboards—in fact, all the supplies and equipment she had requisitioned—had been shipped from the provincial capital and were due in the barrio on the next mailboat. "You have done a good job here, Miss Inocencio," the visitor said.

"Thank you, Mr. Vidal," she said.

She walked to the porch with him. "If you wouldn't mind, sir," she said, leading the way and closing the door behind her.

"For a newcomer in the service, you are doing well," said Mr. Vidal.

"Thank you, sir. You see . . ."

"I understand. There are things, of course, one just can't manage."

"That's just it, sir." said Miss Inocencio. "If I were a man . . . well, in an out of the way place like this, it's hard to be a woman, sir."

She felt she had to say it. If Mr. Vidal should find something wrong in the way she ran the school, he would not blame her too readily. As provincial school inspector, he could be strict with her.

"Aren't the barrio people cooperative enough?" Mr. Vidal asked.

"I can't complain about them, sir."

"You'll find things much easier later on . . . and perhaps for the same reason that you find them difficult now."

She was pleased with this remark. She felt she was making a fair if not indeed a good impression on the school inspector. He would give her an excellent efficiency rating, and perhaps . . . but, oh, how could she think of it? She was hardly three weeks in the service, and a mere substitute at that. Still, I would like to be well thought of, she told herself. Aloud, she said: "Take the case of the garden, sir." She leaned against the porch rail so that she would cut a charming figure. "I had a plan all worked out." She smiled at him.

"Now what about the garden?"

She persevered. "I had a plan, sir, to spare the children much of the work. The grounds, for instance. It's like an old abandoned rice field, sir. It's a man-sized job to put things into shape."

In the classroom several girls were busy mopping the floor. The sound that they made dragging and pushing the desks about the unnailed floor boards reminded Miss Inocencio of the makeshift work that the barrio carpenters had done.

"What do you have in mind?" Mr. Vidal said.

"First of all, I want the garden cleared," she replied. "Cleared of wild grass, and fenced. Five hired men can do the work. The well . . . it's an old one, sir . . . can be made useful again."

With hands clasped behind him, his heavy leather shoes creaking faintly, Mr. Vidal walked the length of the porch and back again. "I see," he said, and stopped abruptly. "That's a good idea. You have good ideas, and that's what we need in the service. Ideas! You should get a permanent appointment."

"Thank you, sir," said Miss Inocencio. "You see, sir, I'm only thinking of the children's welfare."

"Very good. I should say, though, that the barrio is lucky to have the school opened," said Mr. Vidal. "There aren't enough funds, you know. Well, it's worth the money."

"Do you mean, sir, that this is temporary? That you might close the school, sir?"

"Not that I could close it," said Mr. Vidal. "I have no power to do that. But I can send up a memorandum."

"How dreadful!" Miss Inocencio put her hand over her mouth. "Please don't ever do that, sir."

"Much depends on you," said Mr. Vidal.

"I'll do my best. I promise, sir," said Miss Inocencio. "Did you see the building before, sir, shortly after the Occupation?"

"No, but I heard it was used as a Japanese garrison."

Now she must tell him. "There was thick soot in one corner, right over there . . . where the *Ponjap* brewed tea, sir. And, of course, they used desks and floor boards for firewood. Also they had some prisoners here . . . guerrillas, sir . . . among them boys from this barrio, too."

His nostrils quivering, Mr. Vidal looked solemnly around. "Then it was here Mr. Malabanan's son was killed?" he asked.

Miss Inocencio hesitated, surprised at this turn to the conversation. "Yes," she said at last.

"And the family never quite believes it, even now."

"Quite so, sir."

"He was an only son. Did you know him?"

"Pepito Malabanan, sir?"

"That's the name, all right!" Mr. Vidal snapped thumb and forefinger. "The father hasn't given up hope, nor has Mrs. Malabanan. Only this noon, at lunch, they were asking me if it was true some guerrillas in the Panay Regiment had escaped and joined the Regulars. Someday Pepito will be here . . . that's their belief. Do you think it's ever possible . . . his being alive, his ever coming home?"

"I can't say, sir."

"The old couple are very kind. And they think well of you," Mr. Vidal said. He started to walk down the steps. "I understand you're joining us at supper. Mrs. Malabanan's making my visit here as pleasant as possible."

46

"Thank you for coming to our barrio, sir," she said.

On returning to the room to see what her girls had done, Miss Inocencio felt ill at ease. She looked at the window and watched Leoncio and the other boys cutting the *kogon* in the garden. What stayed long in her mind afterwards was Mr. Vidal then turning a street corner and disappearing behind a tall bamboo fence. He had waved his hand casually, as if to say: "I'm a friend, really. Not an officious school official."

Now that the school inspector had gone, the girls began to chatter like parrots as they worked in the classroom. For Miss Inocencio, this was a relief. The girls seemed unusually gay. Clara, aged ten, began to sing a tune, "The Banana Heart," swinging in wide arcs across the torn blackboard an old eraser in her hand. The tune had been Pepito Malabanan's favorite no more than it had been that of every youth and maiden in the barrio. Yet Miss Inocencio could well have claimed the song as his own. He had serenaded her with a guitar many a time and often had sung that plaintive song before her window—this of nights in April and May, before the war. "But I must not think of him any more," she told herself, as she tidied up her desk, pulled out her lesson plan book and uncapped her pen, wondering how best to conduct the next day's class. Certainly there ought to be something new, something no one had done before, something not in the approved course of study which would benefit the children. But would the service allow for originality? Right there before her was the official paperbound outline; already it was checking on her thoughts.

The other girls were teasing Clara. "Look at her, Ma'am . . . as though we had a school program!"

"It's quite all right, girls," Miss Inocencio said.

Whereupon Clara confronted her classmates belligerently, thrusting out her tongue at them. In a minute, pieces of chalk, rags, and erasers flew about the room.

"Stop it!" Miss Inocencio cried.

But no sooner had she raised her voice than contrition seized her. Why shouldn't she let the children alone? Verily, because she felt such a full-fledged woman now and had found a livelihood? Maybe she was begrudging them their innocence. And her next step? To marry and raise a family.

This thought sent her wondering whether Mr. Vidal had a family of his own. Did he have a pretty wife? Two children, maybe—a girl and a boy? And where could Pepito Malabanan be? "I know, Matilde, I should know. I'm his mother. You can't feel what I feel. Pray for his safe return. Our dear Lord will grant it, if only we pray."

Some details of the conversation at school set her wondering whether she had said to Mr. Vidal the right things. It was possible, she thought, that the old couple had told him about her betrothal. For, otherwise, why did Mr. Vidal bring up the subject? But, of course, the fault had been hers; she had mentioned the war. "Did you see how the building looked before, sir?"—and all from an entirely different motive. Perhaps Mr. Vidal had thought she had meant to let him know. Well, then, what would he make of her now? Ah, here's a young woman who's truly in love. Hm! Or would he say instead: How stupid of her! To be quite unable to deal with what's done and over with! What a pity, too, for she's such a pretty creature!

She laid her pen and books away, found no fault with the girls' work and bade them go home. As for the boys and what they had accomplished during the afternoon, she'd go down to the garden herself and see.

48

What had once been wilderness was now cleared land, for the boys had matched their eagerness with industry. Leoncio, who oversaw the work, began cutting away some brush where the well stood rimmed with blocks of soft stone. His trimming revealed the notches for the windlass and the grey lichen upon the blocks of stone. For a good look at the water below, Miss Inocencio leaned over, taking great care not to soil her dress. She held her head for a minute over the dark pit and almost instantly began to feel faint and had to draw away. It was as if the darkness into which she had peered was like a pool where someday she would drown.

To shake off the feeling, she joined the boys. They had to make way for her and were gathered now awaiting to be commended for their efforts. They had done enough for the day, she told them. There was always tomorrow, she might have added; but as though of their own volition her feet took her back to the schoolhouse. She walked away as if in a trance.

The clock atop the empty bookcase was dead. She looked at it and it said nothing to her. Time could well have stopped. She picked up her books and was startled by footsteps— someone was at the porch. She thought Mr. Vidal had returned, but it was only Clara.

"May I carry your books, Ma'am?"

"But I thought you'd gone home," Miss Inocencio said. She piled the books on the desk. "Thank you, Clara. Tell me. Who taught you that song?"

The girl paused and smiled, pleased perhaps by her interest. "My Uncle Pepito, Ma'am," the girl said.

"Oh, yes, I keep forgetting." And an access of tenderness for the girl possessed her. "You are his niece, aren't you?" Miss Inocencio said.

They left the classroom together. As they descended the porch steps, they were met by shrill cries from the garden. A second burst of wild shrieks and Leoncio appeared, running as fleet as a deer, holding something in his hand.

"Leoncio!" Miss Inocencio called after the boy. "What's all this?"

But the boy did not heed her. Instead he ran as far away as he could, stopping only where the growths of maguey bordered the school grounds.

Leoncio could not have betrayed Miss Inocencio more mortally. To hide the hurt, she asked the other boys: "What was that in his hand?"

They watched him in the sun, alone at the edge of the field. The wind stirred the maguey leaves behind him. Leoncio stood there, regarding them proudly. Then, as though bearing a chalice, he walked toward them.

"It's a skull, Ma'am," said one of the boys.

The other boys were quick to indict Leoncio. "We told him, Ma'am, not to go into the well."

Upon a sheaf of kogon grass that lay at Miss Inocencio's feet, Leoncio laid the skull gently. They all fell silent for a moment. The boy stared at his feet, like a prisoner in dock. His lips began trembling perceptibly before he could speak.

"It's Magtanggol's skull, Ma'am . . . Mr. Malabanan's son. That's how they called him."

"What do you know about all this?" Miss Inocencio asked sternly.

"I know, Ma'am," the boy replied. "I know," he repeated earnestly.

The little girl Clara tugged nervously at Miss Inocencio's dress.

Against the yellow-green sheaf of grass, the skull took on a dark blue color, like some piece of metal upon which time had left its mark. There was a haughty anonymity to it; the hollow sockets eloquently suggested no name.

Miss Inocencio bent over to pick up the skull from the cradle of grass where Leoncio had laid it to rest. She could not have explained it away, but the impulse had been too strong. The skull seemed heavy and her hands unsteady. The boys gathered around her in a tight circle. Her hands trembled so, and the skull fell to the ground, breaking in three pieces. Kneeling, she gathered the pieces together.

At half past six that evening, she went to old Mr. Malabanan's house. It was the only frame house in the barrio; its galvanized iron roof, even now in the thickening dusk, rose pale white against the coconut palms.

Mr. Vidal met her at the front steps and, as he stood there in the dark, his first words were: "Do you think it would be possible to identify the skull?"

She was taken aback. "I don't know, sir," she replied. She surmised that on their way home the boys had spread the news. Wrapping up the skull carefully in a handkerchief, she had taken it to the schoolroom and placed it on the topmost shelf of the bookcase. Now it was with some effort that she confessed, "I don't know what to do, sir."

"I knew you had a problem when I heard about it," Mr. Vidal said. "I discussed the matter with Mr. Malabanan immediately. Well, as to whose it is . . . that's not important, really. But I suggested that an urn be made and appropriate prayers said."

They sat there on the porch, a table with a potted plant between them. "What did Mrs. Malabanan say, sir?" Miss Inocencio's eyes brightened.

"The old mother herself agreed to having a *rosario;* no one will claim that we educated people are disrespectful toward the dead." Mr. Vidal rested the back of his chair against the porch wall. "I suggested that the priest in the next town be sent for; as a matter of fact I offered my horse. Interment will be left for the padre to decide."

As he began to rock his chair gently, Miss Inocencio found herself at a loss for what to say. She was indebted enough to him: she saw that much. In his own kind of chivalry, he had anticipated her weakness and spared her some pain.

Three women came up to the house, and after a respectful "Good evening, Mr. School Inspector," and "Good evening, Lady Schoolteacher," they wiped their bare feet upon the *coir* doormat, took off their black kerchiefs, and filed quietly into the *sala*.

"Don't you think I should join them?" Miss Inocencio asked.

She stood up and was about to go, but Mr. Vidal detained her. "Before I forget, I meant to ask you whether you took a subscription to *Teachers' Journal*. It's a requirement of the service, you understand, that teachers subscribe to at least one professional magazine. In a forthcoming issue, incidentally," Mr. Vidal went on, "I've contributed an article entitled 'The Barrio Schools of Tomorrow.' "

"I shall read the article, sir," said Miss Inocencio.

He got up and bowed as she stood to leave; and, later, as she walked across the sala it seemed to her that he was watching her every step with secret admiration.

The family altar was in Mrs. Malabanan's bedroom, and Miss Inocencio felt embarrassed, for the rosario had already started. More than that, the smell of homemade candles, the old women at prayer, old Mr. and Mrs. Malabanan kneeling, humbling before the fact that was Death—these brought upon her, for she had come on tiptoe, an access of depression. Only a cold hand actually clutching her heart could possibly have produced this peculiar effect. Her lips trembling, she knelt and joined in the prayer.

A waft of wind from an open window sent a chill down the

nape of her neck. Then the room began to turn and turn. The walls to her left seemed to be on the point of caving in. Only the altar before her remained steady.

In a trice, the grip upon her heart relaxed. Now she could breathe more easily. Tears moistened her eyes, and for no reason at all she remembered the little girl Clara and her song. She looked up at the lighted altar once more, at the image of the Virgin Mary, at the wooden urn with the blue skull. She rose from her knees, resolved to be free of her past. She got up, thinking: "If I am really free, then no one will mind my leaving this room."

She walked away wondering whether anyone would in censure turn around to watch her go. As she had joined them, so did she now desire to quit their company.

The first thing she heard as she crossed the sala was the rustle of the leaves of the coconut palms across the street. Surely, she thought, the palms were waving their fronds in jubilation over her release.

A freedom too easily won? She was panting when she reached the porch. Mr. Vidal was again rocking his chair. Also, he had lit a cigarette. On seeing her, he got up and offered her his chair.

"Thank you," she said, still out of breath. But she did not sit down.

"It's too bad I'm not a praying man. Otherwise, I would have joined you." Mr. Vidal was chuckling softly. Then in a more serious vein, "Out here in the dark, I've been thinking about your work. I realize your handicaps. No professional associations, no books, no magazines. This is a God-forsaken place! What chances has one for self-improvement here?"

She leaned upon the porch rail and looked at the silhouettes of the palm trees, slim and dark shapes against the yet darker sky.

"I was wondering," Mr. Vidal continued, "whether the

School Board has sent you to the wrong place. I'll mention the subject in my memorandum."

Mr. Vidal flung his cigarette away, underscoring the finality of the matter. Then he drew her to him; it was as if after having fled from the other room she had flung herself into his arms. Momentarily shocked, she felt the hum of the prayers in the other room come to her in a sudden crescendo, as if she had stepped directly upon the path of a horde of angry bees.

"Perhaps you'd consider a transfer to a much bigger school?" Mr. Vidal continued. "There's a vacancy at the provincial capital. Yes, why not?"

The kindness in his voice did not escape her, yet she could say nothing in turn. She became tongue-tied, wary over this prospect of being his protegeé.

"Perhaps during the vacation you'd like to attend Summer Institute?"

He placed his arm on her shoulder—a fittingly protective gesture, she believed, so that the barrio and all its fetishes could not lay their claims upon her any more. She let him draw her to him, warmly, closer.

But she heard herself speaking, "It's very kind of you." It was as though someone were making decisions on her behalf. She stepped back, startled, and gave a cold firmness to her voice, "I must stay. . ."

There—her tongue had uttered them! And having said them, she let Mr. Vidal hold her hand when he reached out for it again, but only one minute longer. The dark palms were staring at her.

1950

Where's My Baby Now?

ALTHOUGH FOR THE PAST NINE YEARS MRS. BILBAO has had nothing to conceal from her husband, she feels she must keep this one a secret. To speak about the matter will be embarrassing, to say the least. How will she begin? And having begun, and persevered, what of this thing which she will not succeed in confiding to him. Bilbao is a busy man; a freelance accountant can be a very busy man. And he's the quiet type: you can hardly tell what's behind all the diligence he observes going through the musty books of some small merchant trying to avoid his taxes. Such hours he keeps at times at some downtown office stuffy with the smell of ink and typewriter oil; and towards the twentieth or twenty-first of the month, how he sweats it out in some dingy mezzanine in the company of a pale little nervous bookkeeper who exudes from some secret spot under his shirt the aroma of imported cigarettes. Then, for an entire week, Bilbao is grubby and sullen, a dull fire smouldering in his eyes.

She can't understand it. But she must admit he's a wizard at budgeting his time, so much so he can find two or three hours each day for watching the children in the courtyard, the while ostensibly going over some baker's balance sheet or some ice-cream parlor's journal-ledger. Mrs. Bilbao thinks this is rather unusual. No man ought to take such interest in the games children play.

She will have to think, forgetting the children's convenience entirely, about moving out to a new neighborhood. For there's nothing here for her, nothing to speak of. Unless, of course, you can feel nice about the streets in this part of the city being named after flowers.

Theirs is Apartment 177-F, Jasmine Street, the sixth from the gate. A thoughtful man, the landlord has built an adobe wall around the block, anticipating perhaps that some day his tenants may elect to keep away from all society. And there's the courtyard, too, for the children. Although hardly fifteen feet wide, it's covered with smooth concrete with trapezoids and triangles of varying sizes simulating flagstones, thanks to some fanciful mason. The one feature Mrs. Bilbao approves of is the length of water-pipe like an inverted U, at the end of the courtyard, from which a grill door swings stiffly upon its hinges; and it's the fresh purple paint, so fetching in the morning sun, of which she's really proud.

She couldn't say that others feel the same way. The Poncianos, for instance. Well, perhaps they can feel good about other things. They occupy 117-A, the apartment nearest the street, and thus enjoy the advantage of having two extra windows. But this is offset by their having to serve as gatekeepers *ex officio*. If they are annoyed over this, they do not indeed show it. On coming home in the late evenings, Bilbao has to call out loud to Pedro, one of their servants, to request that the bolt be unfastened. Being the person he is, her husband, Mrs. Bilbao thinks, approves of the Poncianos' preferring this service to their risking the chance of a burglar's visit. Pedro, the servant, having allowed Bilbao to enter, slips in the bolt for the night, clamping on the lock that he has been carrying in his pocket all day and then shuffling away, his brow lifted with an air of fulfillment.

The pleasures of this life are so few and far between you have to snatch them perforce? Her husband is very pleased with this arrangement over the gate, it is true. "The children will be safe this way," he says. They have three of them, two of kindergarten age. And the courtyard, he has often remarked, is just the sort of oversized playpen that the young ones need. The landlord, bless his soul, has left a strip of earth shaped like a fat cigar in the center; here some colorful and fragrant rosebush may be grown. But Mr. Bilbao likes it bare; he likes his pleasures all of one kind. The children, says he, can run about more freely. And Mr. Ponciano agrees with him. The Ponciano girls, ages four and six, have led their mother to say, "We needn't worry about them, so long as our Pedro's around to watch the gate." Doubtless, she has in mind the rickety jeeps that cruise up and down Jasmine Street, raising a cloud of dust that has the same thickness, the same consistency always, regardless of the time of day; and although helpless against the dust, the children are spared effectively from those reckless drivers.

Mrs. Bilbao understands all this. What really puzzles her is her husband's interest in the children's games. "Do you know," he says, the legs of his cane chair scraping the cement—he finds working in the mornings in the shade of the wall quite pleasant these days—"do you know? A rumor has spread. There's famine abroad. And the children have made a game of it."

Mrs. Bilbao has brought out her basket of wash. It's no game, in so far as she's concerned; this is Saturday, and she is too busy to listen to this kind of talk.

But Bilbao perseveres. "I recall how it was in my day," he says, having fixed his chair where the sunlight slants so, making huge diamonds of the broken lemonade bottles embedded on top of the adobe bricks. It will not hurt his eyes to sit there and go over several books of Buenas Dias Co., successors to De Luxe Bakery. "Yes, yes," he says, spreading one thick journal before him, his feet propped upon a box. "We need to fly kites, but only during certain months of the year, mind you. After seven, did you play with dolls?" he asked her suddenly. "Children make good prophets, you know."

57

The impertinence, the impudence of it! He knows she has work to do, a clothesline to fasten properly. There's the nail on the wall to which she can tie the line, but to do this properly she must stand on that chair, better yet, on that box. But does he offer to help? Instead, he asks again, "After seven, did you still play with dolls?"

"I don't remember," she says, concealing her petulance.

"And when was it you played Man and Wife? And House-keeping, let's say."

"I don't recall. And I don't care to," she says reaching for the nail on the clammy wall—because if there's a will there's a way.

Then, uncoiling the clothesline after her, she crosses to the other side of the court. Here the drain pipe is on the same level as that rail; and he need not help. No. There ought to be no need for him, ever. There's one hopeless fellow for you; he keeps asking—"When? When?" Instead of asking "What's next?" he pesters you with "Do you remember? Do you recall? Why, in my day . . ." He speaks as though he were sixty, a retired cigar-smoking bureau chief, on a fat pension.

She hangs the wash, trappings that have survived the years, upon the line. His white shirts (he loves white), her chemises and slips, the children's clothes, then the sheets that had been soiled the night before. "Here, can't you help a bit?" she calls, for the first sheet is heavy and causes the line to sag.

Mr. Bilbao pushes the wooden box from under his feet. There's some chivalry left in him after all. With a trembling arm, she props the line tentatively. "Quick! Give me a hand!"

He's so sweet about it. He has run to the house and brought back the long broomstick that the maid Concha fashioned against the day for sweeping cobwebs off the kitchen ceiling and the back-porch eaves.

"There, does it work? It does!"

"Thanks."

But at what price! You've to listen more to talk, and it's not about the clothesline, either.

"The courtyard is bare now. The effects of the rumor are evident. Not only have the children forgotten hopscotch, they have put their other toys away. The tricycles are gone; the four-wheeled wagon belonging to the clubfoot at 117-D is gone."

"What does it all mean?" she asks, bringing out the second sheet, soap-suddy white in the basket. "Give me a hand!"

"What does it mean? Why, I used to be pleasantly disturbed in my work. You remember the children used to play ball. 'Safe! Safe!' they'd shout, in the midst of their game, really softball simplified, with two bases instead of four, at which Pedro presides both as umpire and retriever, for the ball often rolls off to the street. But now my mornings have become quiet. You do not know about this; you're often out of the house."

That's the first of his many hints. For the moment, she must hide her feelings.

"And, also, the children used to play a game called Storekeeper. The favorite place for it used to be the front of 177-C. There the children gather in the shade of the wall, our own as well as the Ponciano and Gomez children. Somebody plays storekeeper, with the Chinese who owns the general store at the street corner for their model. I used to pause in my work to watch. They have their own version of buying and selling, of haggling, of getting into debt, of holding up the storekeeper for a grain of garlic or a bulb of onion. Pedro says it's that way with some characters in the neighborhood; they make it their business to mortify the Chinese. I'm surprised you've never observed this. Never?"

He insists on an answer. Impatient with him herself, she relents. "No, I've noticed nothing at all," she says, stretching the white sheet upon the line, right between the wall and her frillies.

"You're away much too often," he says with a smile so innocent as to seem without malice. "But just watch them mornings when they're back from kindergarten."

That's how it is. He gets the children involved. It is somewhat difficult to nourish her petulance into disgust, and, under the circumstances, perhaps into hate.

"Now, give me a hand! And don't be so clumsy, please. There, careful now!"

And it's all her fault. So says that look in his eyes. She ought to have known better. She ought not to have moved the prop so, making the line more taut.

"Concha! Concha!"

The girl must rinse the sheets again. There she is at the door, and she peeks at the sunshine and runs, runs, runs, runs to Mr. Bilbao's rescue—with not a look of protest in that servant-face.

Bilbao's is expressionless, almost an indifferent face. Mrs. Bilbao confronts it calmly. "You've to fix the line yourself."

"It was bound to snap," he says, picking up the loose ends. Then, as he begins to knot them, "Why, in the old days you could get genuine clotheslines . . . not this kind . . . I was speaking about this new game of the children's . . . was watching them the other afternoon, you know. Where were you then? At some meeting or other? Which was this one, now?"

"The Mother's Civic League," she replies.

"I was there, watching . . . was telling Mrs. Ponciano, across the courtyard, that her eldest boy will perhaps grow up to be a leader. For there he was, urging the children to till

60

the strip at the center. Then, there they planted corn . . . no, simply sticks at first. Later, Pedro came with real corn . . . goodness knows where he got it. The children, gathering about him thinking he had something other than familiar boiled peanuts in that tiny paper bag for them, began digging into his pockets. You should have been here. Pedro might have stood there all morning, himself a seven-year-old all over, with the zeal of the giver burning in his eyes— There, you've as good a knot as can be made with this string."

Mrs. Bilbao watches him stretch the clothesline to a new tautness. For him, this must seem truly an admirable accomplishment. Suddenly she feels tender towards this man who is her husband, this man for whom she has borne three children. But a mother's instincts are beyond cavil. You cannot reason down a woman's fears. And Mrs. Bilbao fears that three children establish her claim to motherhood quite eloquently. Whether it is an angel or the spirit of God itself in her blood that cries "Enough! Enough!" she does not know. But it is a stern and urgent voice, with its one stern and urgent message. A mother listens with her heart.

As if she hasn't been listening to his talk—must she admit it?—a sentiment, nevertheless, escapes her. "Sometimes I can't help feeling sorry for the children," she says. "Why, as a child . . ." No, she corrects herself, "as a girl . . . on a farm . . ."

It is her favorite memory. She's afraid, lest she launches upon a more substantial evocation of a childhood long since gone, irrecoverable like pin money squandered on some trifle in a bazaar.

"Now give me a hand," she says, for Concha has returned with the sheets.

"I've it from Mrs. Ponciano that once in a while the children refuse to eat. Part of their game . . . they'll carry it as far as that, you see . . . and I've been waiting for it. They'll bring pails of water out here, and cry out loud 'Flood! Flood!'— meaning the waters have washed away the fields, the crops are gone, and there'll be hunger everywhere."

Mrs. Bilbao can't help laughing, the fun bubbling from deep within her. So this is why he sits there! Well, if it pleases him, let him be.

She remembers that the children will be home from kindergarten. It's no matter. She must hurry off, this time to that symposium on Progressive Education. These lectures and civic club activities are her only bid for widening her horizon. And there are several in the offing, now that the town's full of visiting American professors.

She picks up her clothes basket, which is too large for tucking in under her arm like a book, and starts for the apartment. But Mr. Bilbao, now back in his chair, feet propped once more upon the empty box, detains her.

"I've heard the Ponciano children have amassed a supply of biscuits," he starts all over again, his eyes on the empty baskets at her side. "The father has been in the habit of bringing home two-pound tins of biscuits, which he's fond of himself; and no sooner is he at the gate than his little girls rush for the present, and without so much as a 'Thank you, Papa,' they run to the house with this fresh addition to their stock. I've Mrs. Ponciano's word; the girls have in her closet a pyramid of red-yellow and cellophane-sealed tins of 'Eat Well Brand. Made in U.S.A.' biscuits. 'That high already!' she says, blushing."

"And you're waiting, hoping to see those little girls harass their father again?"

"Exactly," Mr. Bilbao says calmly, "if you want to put it that way."

How exasperating! And with Bennie and Bobby home

now, the girl's pink dimity pinafore no more soiled than the boy's sailor suit. "What? You home already?" But it is as though she had said: "This is my cue. Now I must go."

"Oh, no, darling! You'll spoil my dress." Mrs. Bilbao retreats, warily, to spare the really stunning thing she has on, for Bennie's embrace can be disastrous. The dress is of fine linen; the Chinese collar makes her ever so attractive. "Now be a good girl," she says.

Yet, in a moment, she presses her cheeks upon Bobby's (because he is her favorite, although he looks every inch like his father) and then upon Bennie's. "Go wipe yourself with a towel," she tells the girl, for Bennie has brought home with her the familiar aroma of Jasmine Street sunshine.

Mr. Bilbao drags his cane chair back to the house. "You have this other luncheon meeting?" he asks, and then turning to the children: "Oh, Bennie, Bobby . . . now tell Daddy what you've learned in school today . . ."

It's a ceremony which, Mrs. Bilbao knows, is more a matter of form than of substance. The upshot of it will be that the two-year-old, who's been serenely asleep all this while, will soon be sniveling in his wet bed.

"Hssshh!" she exhorts them, peeking from the bedroom door at the tiny bed in the corner. "Johnny's still asleep. And it's the Women's Social Action Committee, Daddy. I've forgotten to tell you." She says "Daddy" with a special flair, for the children's sake. They will know, they're bound to. She adds, even more casually yet, "And after the meeting, that other symposium I've mentioned. (Has she, indeed, told him?) Some congressmen will be present."

Now how stuffy the house seems! Has she suddenly filled it with imaginary people—congressmen, lecturers, members of the WSAC? She crosses the sala and the dining room, escaping to the kitchen at last.

Now, the last-minute instructions for Concha. There's an extra bottle of milk for Johnny-boy in the refrigerator—he'll need that soon. The maid must heat some sausages for the children's lunch; those finger-shaped ones will do, leftovers from breakfast though they are. "Times are hard, Concha. Never waste the slightest scrap. And mind the faucet. We still have the water bill to pay."

She is aware that she has become Good Housekeeping and Vigilance personified. Efficiency and a high sense of responsibility exude from her like Heavenly Colonial, say; or some such imported perfume which, though but sparingly used, keeps its scent for an agreeably long time, enhancing the realization—the fulfillment, even—of womanhood.

It is this thought that propels her out of the kitchen, which after all is really Concha's world. Bennie and Bobby, their necks flushed from rubbing with the towel, are waiting for their father at the doorway. Mr. Bilbao has brought out Johnny-boy: the two-year-old has been wide awake, it seems, these past five minutes at least. But what a well-disposed little fellow. He ought to whine as most children do on getting up from bed. But there he is, perched so proudly upon his Daddy's arm, his soft cheek against Daddy's cavernous nostrils.

For she feels jealous of Daddy. And it's Mr. Bilbao the accountant, not Daddy at all, who, now with a smile, holds the door open for her.

There's a distinction there. In applause for the thought, the bright sunshine in the courtyard sweeps upon her white linen dress, lays siege upon her in a transport of rapture. She makes three—four—careless steps. Then suddenly she remembers. She must have a more studied and purposive air.

She tries it—head held high, arms swinging artfully, cutting across some imaginary ribbon before her. There, directly in front of her leatherette belt! And the small black purse tightly clasped in her one hand. Down, down the length of the courtyard, and she knows with each pressure of her heels that the flagstones are what they really are.

Mr. Bilbao's wheedling voice, which seems to belong to some aspect of his nature that she has never quite discovered, reaches her. He's chanting, "Say bye-bye to Mummie. Say bye-bye."

But Johnny-boy only squints at the sunshine. And from Bobby and Bennie, who are much older and can therefore be trusted to understand: "Bye-bye, Mummie,"—Daddy there at their side, their shy voices clear across the courtyard.

She cannot open her palm (it's the hand with the purse) as she waves to the children. Actually, she is describing an arc with her fist.

Scenes like this are a concession she must give. She must be impartial with her love, such as it is. She doubts whether she loves Daddy as Daddy at all: is it middle-age creeping in? All the same, it's her wish to be always one step ahead: after such words at the lectures as *troglodytical* and *archetype,* how self-conscious and yet how alert and aware one can become: it can't now be said that, although a mere housewife, she isn't progressive—this fact she feels has become the essence of her life—and to be forever interested in the significant and new, to be always in search of facts, to investigate and evaluate that other beautiful world and not to sit there watching children all day long at some odd game but rather to cut the heart open and probe into its secrets—.

1950

Come and Go

ONE MORNING IN OCTOBER 1940, FELIPE (ALIAS Philip) Bautista, thirty-six, steward third class, U. S. Naval Transport Service, arrived in Buenavista on the *Nuestra Senora del Carmen* for a brief visit with his family. He had neither written nor sent a wire. He had done this on purpose—to Nanay, letters had somehow meant serious money troubles, and telegrams had never been anything but ruthless messengers of death. With a notice from the North American Life Assurance Co. of Toronto in hand, she once spent an afternoon wandering all over town, seeking out relatives and friends for counsel, not being quite able to bring herself to believe that anyone in the world could possibly have the kindness to offer her two thousand pesos just because Papa had died. Yet that was exactly what the letter said. She had walked home with a heavy heart, shaking her head, unable to comprehend the disguises of providence.

Philip had not found this amusing at all, although in a quite longish letter of Perla's that had reached him in San Francisco, she had said that it was just that. And to think that Nanay was now five years dead, Philip told himself. It was pointless to ask what she would say about this visit, but he couldn't help thinking of her. Surely, were she alive, she would wish that he had brought along some presents for the family.

Unfortunately, he had bought his ticket on impulse; but realizing that he had no time to shop, he might have managed to buy a bag or two of oranges and mangoes from the rowdy fruit peddlers at the pier. The family would understand, he now hoped; and by family, Philip meant merely his

66

sister Perla, whom he had not seen for thirteen years, and her husband, whom he knew only by name.

He had not expected anyone to meet him at the wharf and, though the crowd was large and the air rang with suddenly familiar greetings in Bisayan, he did find no one there to welcome him. He reminded himself that there were but ninety tons of copra to load up from the Stevenson warehouse; he might allow two hours for this. Promptly afterward, he figured, the ship would weigh anchor for the return voyage to Manila.

A short walk across the town plaza and past the market place, and he was home. And this then was Perla, the "Perls" of those letters he had posted from such odd places as Baltimore, Port Niches, and Vancouver. She had run up the porch, crying. "Oh, *manong,* you almost scared me!"—and what with the children gathered about her, she looked like Nanay all over, the Nanay of long ago, before he had put the two poles of the earth between them.

"This must be Rebby," he said, holding the feet of the baby that Perls carried astride her hip, exactly as Nanay in her day might carry a ten-month-old. "Did I scare you also, Rebby?" he asked. Her feet were the softest things he had held in a long time.

Jerking her legs, Rebby gave out a shrill, tremulous cry. "But it's your Uncle Philip!" said Perls and, turning to him, explained: "She's just now cutting her teeth. That's why she's so bad-tempered . . . and this is Sid," she added, drawing gently from behind her the little girl clinging to the Mother Hubbard that made Perls look like a long-widowed fishwife. "You be quiet, you!" she threatened, slapping Rebby on the thigh. "You've come on the *Carmen?* It's already six. My, we must have breakfast soon. Ruuuuudy! Ruuuuuuuuuddddddyyyyyy!" she called. But no one answered. "He must have gone for the bread already. That boy minds his chores."

So this is the family—the thought kept coming like a refrain. And this, the house—a three-room frame house set on the side of the rock-covered hill overlooking the harbor. Here it was, complete with the strip of graveled road for frontage and the embankment that kept the sea away at high tide. The porch, not yet washed dry by the morning sunshine, had the dank odor that exuded from those rocks and the soursop trees in the yard.

Perls led the way into the *sala* and opened the windows that framed, each of them, a view of the wharf and the interisland steamer moored alongside. Beside the Stevenson warehouse rose the hill of copra from whence a hundred stevedores or so, like hungry ants blessed with a pile of sugar, hurried off to the ship, the brown sacks on their sweat-soaked and glistening bodies.

Philip wanted to enjoy the scene, for it recalled something from his boyhood. But Perls led him away to show him the room where Papa and Nanay had died. The four-poster with its sagging *bejuco* weave, except perhaps for the torn sheet that Ruddy had slipped out of, seemed exactly as Philip had seen it last. On the floor was the *buri* mat over which a green-and-red-checkered mosquito bar hung; here, then, Perls and the two children slept. From here she had dragged out Rebby and Sid to answer the pounding at the door.

"I didn't recognize your voice," Perls confessed, laughing. "Fermin . . . that's my husband . . . is with us only three nights of the week. I thought you were somebody from Agsawa with bad news."

"And what does he do in Agsawa? That's on the other side of the island, isn't it?"

"That's where he teaches. He's been banished, you know. And he has not been well . . . asthma . . . perhaps worsened by his going up and down the steep mountain road."

"I hope he gets better," Philip said, feeling suddenly injured and angry, even, at how luck had cheated his sister. She ought to have found somehow a much healthier man for a husband. That would have been a relief, at least. Philip had no idea how this fellow Fermin looked, never having seen even a picture of him. The name itself didn't sound right; Philip imagined a thin, long-necked creature of forty, with a wheezing in his throat at each gulp of rain-fresh mountain air.

"Friday nights, that's when he's here. It's a three-hour hike. Then he goes back early Monday morning."

"That's difficult," Philip said.

"We can't join him because Rudy's in grade six. Besides, somebody has to stay in this house."

"Perhaps things will turn out right in the end," Philip said, lamely. He had taken off his gabardine jacket and hung it on the back of the rattan chair.

"I hope so," Perls said.

"And how old are you, Sid?" Philip asked his niece, telling himself, "You can't bear the children any grudges. You mustn't, anyway."

"Six," the girl said, in English.

"You're in school already? Which grade?"

"Two," the girl said, holding up two fingers of her right hand.

"Rebby's really fourteen months now," Perls said. "You will stay till Saturday, maybe? That's three days at least."

"I can't," said Philip. "I must get back, on that boat over there," and he pointed to the *Carmen* quietly sitting at the wharf.

"Then you'll not meet him . . . Fermin, I mean."

"I'm sorry."

"You can't stay, really?"

"I have to return to my ship by tomorrow evening. I'm lucky enough to have this leave."

"Why? Will there be a war? People here talk a lot about it," Perls said. "That's why I keep telling my husband, 'Don't feel so bad about things. This is not yet the worst,' I said to him."

"Maybe you're right," Philip admitted.

"But we'll be safe here? What do you think?" Perls asked, nervously. Philip noticed she kept patting Rebby on the back, perhaps to conceal her anxiety.

"You shouldn't worry," said Philip.

"The war will be far away?"

"Maybe," Philip began, but decided not to continue. The transport USNS *Harold Tilyard Matson* had brought fresh units of the 61st Infantry to Manila, but he couldn't tell his sister that. He had expected her to ask: What then? What will happen? Will you be safe? But Perls was doubtless wrapped up in her own small troubles. Husband away in some God-forsaken station, and with asthma and all that. Rebby undernourished. Rudy and Sid to keep in school. Old house to look after. He understood the facts, but something rankled inside him. The name Fermin . . . that was it! It grated in his ears.

A strange mood prodded his thoughts back to those days when he had begged Papa and Nanay for permission to go to America. It pained him to remember the trouble he had caused. Winning Nanay over had been difficult. In his desperation, he had resorted to acting like a blackguard in high school—picking fights, insulting the history teacher, openly challenging the principal to a nine-round boxing bout. From all the trouble he had caused, it seemed quite clear that, as a growing disgrace to the family, he ought to be away and out of sight.

Raising the money for his fare had not been easy, either. It had to be steerage, but even then Papa had to mortgage his five-hectare coconut grove in Bankalanan. It was three years later that Papa died, and to Philip was sent half of the insurance money so that he might return home. The question had not been, return home to what? but, rather, with what? A year in Hawaii, two summers in Alaska, and, in between, dreary months among the farms of Fresno. His pride told him he could not go back with only stories about the poolrooms in Sacramento for the folks. Nor would they be satisfied with even the choicest secrets of the *sikoy-sikoy* joints of San Francisco.

He wrote fewer and fewer letters. It was only after Nanay's death, he remembered, that he had hit on the nickname "Perls." A correspondence began which, if desultory, took account of Fermin and the children, one after another as they came. In some way all of them became, for Philip, more than ten thousand miles away, somewhat real people.

"Come, Sid. Sit here by me," he called to the little girl and made room for her on the chair.

But she drew away. Philip noticed for the first time the dress she wore; it looked like an undershirt that maybe her brother had discarded five years before.

"It's your own Uncle Philip, Sid," her mother reminded the girl.

"Let me give you five dollars," he said, pulling out his wallet. He flicked the crisp note before handing it to the girl. "Buy yourself a dress."

"But Philip!" Perls protested. "You may not have enough yourself."

"Who? Me?" he laughed.

"And what do you say to your Uncle Philip?"

Sid stepped forward but kept her eyes to the floor. "Thank you, Uncle," she said.

"Bright girl! And here's another five dollars for Rebby," said Philip. "Look, Rebby," he said, touching the little one's cheek with his forefinger. "Tell Mama to buy a dress also. Now don't you forget."

"They do really need clothes and shoes," Perls admitted. "The Bankalanan coconuts . . . we paid up the mortgage only three years ago . . . did not bring in enough last quarter. As for Fermin's salary . . . well, you know how that is."

"What about Mama then? Doesn't Mama need anything?" He posed the question to both Rebby and Sid, chuckling, and then looked into his wallet to count the bills still remaining. He pulled out a fifty-dollar note and handed this to Perls.

"Sid," said Perls, "you'd better let me keep your money. You'll only lose it."

"And Rudy? Whatever happened to Rudy?" Philip asked. He felt expansive, relieved of those depressing thoughts, even of the resentments, a while back. "It's Rudy I remember very well." He showed Perls the cellophane leaf in his wallet. "I have been carrying this snapshot all these years. Look, he has Rebby's features . . . the eyes, especially."

Perls looked out the window, craning her neck to see better beyond the point where the embankment turned. "Oh . . . wait . . . there he is now," she said.

Philip took Sid to the window: she was friendly again. He lifted her up so that she could see her brother coming down the road. "Rudy's almost a young man now," Philip said, seeing the barefoot boy with a paper bag in one hand hugged tight to his chest. He was pleased to see that his nephew had his mother's pleasing features—the oval face, the frank eyes, the full and well-shaped lips.

"Rudy," said Perls, as the boy stopped at the door. "Rudy, do you remember your Uncle Philip?"

It was as if the boy was not looking at his mother but at some object beyond. His big, round eyes did not blink.

"What have you told him about me?" Philip asked, suddenly vexed.

"Nothing. Nothing much. Except that last year, especially, he kept looking at maps and asking about you. That was when we received your postcard with the picture of your ship."

The reply soothed Philip a little. "Maybe, when he grows up, he'll also . . ."

"Oh, no. God forbid!" Perls gasped.

The boy rubbed the soles of his feet self-consciously on the doorsill. Then he walked into the room as if, to begin with, he did not know what to do with the bag of bread he had bought.

"Let me have it," said his mother. "You look after Rebby. I'll prepare our breakfast."

"You were as big as Rebby when . . ." but Philip stopped. He was about to tell the boy "when I first read about you." Instead, he showed him the snapshot in his wallet. "Do you know who that is?"

Rudy shook his head slowly.

"But that's you!" Philip said.

"Me?"

"That's you, of course!"

It was only then that Rudy smiled. He carried Rebby awkwardly, and then the baby wet herself. He tried to hold her at arm's length. Philip took Rebby then from him and seated her on his chair.

"She will also wet your chair," said Rudy.

"That's all right," said Philip, keeping Rebby steady. "Tell me, what has your mama told you about me?" he asked quickly, speaking softly.

They could hear Perls in the kitchen. A kettle had crashed to the floor, and the smoke from the woodstove smelled damp. The boy smiled.

"Tell me. What did your mama say about your Uncle Philip?"

"That you were bad."

"What else besides?"

"That you boxed people's ears and then ran away."

Philip laughed. "Your mama, of all people!" he said, enjoying himself. "Now listen, Rudy. You'll come with me to America, will you?" He felt he had to make it up with this boy somehow.

"But I'm too young," Rudy said, his eyes brightening.

"No, not now. When you're older. Look, I'll give you my jacket. Will you try it on?"

The boy fingered the smooth, gray fabric, unbelieving, then swung the jacket over his shoulders. It fell very loose down his neck and shoulders, and in his short pants and with his bony knees and skinny calves, he looked like a scarecrow out of season.

"Maybe next year, it will fit me," Rudy decided, after looking himself over.

"Good," Philip encouraged him. "And here's something else," he said, unfastening the gold watch off his wrist.

"It's for me, really?" Rudy held the bracelet gingerly, afraid that the gold would tarnish at his touch.

"For you," Philip said, now watching the boy wear the timepiece tight up his arm. "Let's tell Mama all about it."

Rebby was unsafe on the chair, and so Philip had to take her away. They had breakfast on the low form in the kitchen. Philip found the board damp and smelly, as though fish broth had been spilled all over and the wood had soaked it in. He sat on the floor and, having rolled up his shirt sleeves, dunked his bread in the chocolate that Perls had prepared. It was not as thick as he would have liked; and he saw that the long-necked brass pot Perls used had fallen to the floor, an arm's length from the woodstove. There was a saucerful of crisp anchovies that Perls had roasted in an old frying pan. There was also some fried rice. He was glad Perls had not brought out anything special.

"Rudy has a coat to wear when he goes to America. He has a watch, too," Philip said, halfway through the meal.

"It's your father who needs a watch, Rudy," said Perls, from where she sat with Rebby on her lap. Perls fed her with chocolate-dunked bread.

"The jacket doesn't fit him now; but, maybe, later . . ." Philip began again.

"It's your father who should be wearing things like that, Rudy. He has school programs and meetings to attend. He can use a coat and look better," said his mother.

"I'll let Papa wear it then," Rudy said. "But it still will be mine, won't it?"

"Of course," his uncle said.

"And Papa may use the watch, but it still belongs to me," the boy pursued.

"Yes, it'll be yours," his uncle said.

"All right. It still will be yours," Perls conceded.

Philip imagined how his jacket would look on his scrawny brother-in-law and wished he had not been so generous to his nephew. He wished the watch would stop ticking the very moment his brother-in-law had it on. He couldn't help asking Perls: "This husband you have, does he take good care of you?"

"How funny you are, Philip," said Perls, putting another piece of bread into Rebby's mouth.

Presently, Rudy got up from the table. Sid followed. Perls was wiping little Rebby's chocolate-smeared face with the hem of the baby's dress when Philip got up and joined his nephew and niece in the sala.

"Look," Rudy cried, dancing before his sister Sid. He had put on his uncle's gabardine jacket again. His arms lost in the long sleeves, Rudy dangled the gold watch, letting it touch his sister's ear now and again, to tease her.

"Mine! All mine!" Rudy said, thumping about. Because he would not let Sid listen to the ticking of the watch long enough to suit her, the poor girl succumbed to tears in her frustration.

The *Carmen* let out a sharp, hissing sound all of a sudden, followed by four taunting blasts.

"Now we have to hurry," said Perls, running to the bedroom.

After the four blasts, the ship's whistle gave out a long and deep, heart-wrenching moan. Rudy looked at his watch.

"Quick, put on your school uniforms," Perls said. She had brought out a little white blouse for Rebby and had changed herself, wearing now a pink, newly pressed cotton dress with little prints of sailboats at the hem. There would be just enough time to see Philip off. From the wharf, Rudy and Sid would have to hurry off to school.

A thin, silver smoke hung over the ship's funnel, lingering there a while. Philip was entranced by it. It rose in the air and slowly transformed into a white silk ribbon, a piece of bunting from the arch of coconuts that crowned the hills beyond, across the bay. Then, in a trice, it was gone.

"That's right," Philip said, softly, as if to himself. "I really have to get back."

Vaguely, he saw where Rudy belonged. Then, more clearly: Friday was not too far away—soon the boy's joys would be over. Already, Perls could count on adding to her fifty dollars the ten from Rebby and Sid. But then all that money would go for clothes, shoes, and the medicines that Fermin—that horrible name!—needed for his asthma. And food, too.

Philip was frightened by his knowledge of Perls's burden, and he was hurt by his own foolish and futile gestures toward making it seem easier to bear. There was the war she feared, and she had not forgotten him altogether. It seemed that his thirteen years of escape from this house had converged upon him for the sole purpose of making him wish Perls had all the strength and courage she needed; and he forgave her the chocolate, her exiled spouse, even the horrid Mother Hubbard. It was not inconceivable after all that someday, out there at sea, he would have to go, like that wisp of smoke, and vanish into nowhere.

1953

The Sea Beyond

THE *ADELA*, A RECONVERTED MINESWEEPER THAT had become the mainstay of commerce and progress in Sipolog Oriental, was on her way to San Roque. As Horacio Arenas, our new assistant, wanted to put it, the *Adela* was "expected" at San Roque, which was the provincial capital, "in seven hours." He spoke at some length of this particular voyage, looking worn-out instead of refreshed after the two-week vacation we had hoped he would enjoy.

There he was, he said, one of the hundred-odd impatient passengers huddled under the low canvas awning of the upper deck. A choppy sea met the ship as she approached Punta Dumadali, and the rise and fall of the deck suggested the labored breathing of an already much-abused beast of burden. Her hatches were in fact quite full, Arenas said. Hundreds of sacks of copra had filled her hold at Dias. Piled all over the lower deck were thousands of pieces of *lauan* boards from the mills of San Tome. The passageways alongside the engine room were blocked by enormous baskets of cassava and bananas. A dozen wild-eyed Simara cows, shoulder to shoulder in their makeshift corral at the stern, mooed intermittently as though the moon-drenched sea were their pasture.

For the moon had risen over the Maniwala Range three miles to the starboard. As more and more the *Adela* rounded the Punta Dumadali, the wind sent the ship bucking wildly. An hour before, all this would have been understandable; it was puzzling, if not thoroughly incomprehensible, now. This kind of sea was unusual, for the Dumadali headland was known to mariners to throw off, especially at this time of year, if at no other, the full force of the *noroeste*. If some explanation were to be sought, it would be in some circumstance peculiar only to this voyage. This was the consensus, which made possible the next thought: that some presence was about, some evil force perhaps—so the talk went on board—which, until propitiated, might yet bring the ship to some foul end. The cows were markedly quiet now. The ship continued to pitch about: whenever the wind managed to tear at the awnings and cause loose ends of the canvas to beat savagely at the wire mesh that covered the railings, small unreal patches of sea glimmered outside in the moonlight.

It was no secret that there was a dying man on board. He was out there in the third-class section. Whatever relation his presence bore to the unpleasantness in the weather no one could explain, but the captain did do something. He had the man moved over to the first-class section, which was less crowded and so would probably be more comfortable for him.

The transfer was accomplished by two members of the crew. They carried the cot on which the man lay, and two women, the man's wife and her mother, followed them. Ample space was cleared for the cot; the women helped push canvas beds and chairs out of the way. Finally, the two men brought their burden down. The ship listed to starboard suddenly, and it seemed that from all quarters of the deck the hundred-odd passengers of the *Adela* let out a wild scream.

Then the ship steadied somehow. For a moment it seemed as if her engines had stopped. There was a gentle splashing sound, as though the bow had clipped neatly through the last of those treacherous waves. Either superior seamanship or luck held sway, but so still were the waters that the ship might have entered then an estuary, the very mouth of an unknown river.

The excitement had roused the passengers and, in the first-class section at least, everyone sat up to talk, to make real all over again the danger they had just been through. The steaming hot coffee which the steward began serving in thick, blue-rimmed cups encouraged conversation. The presence of the two women and the man in their midst was a subject hardly to be overlooked. A thick, gray woolen blanket covered the man all over, except about the face. His groans, underscored by the faint tapping of the wind on the canvas awnings, now became all too familiar. The mother attracted some notice, although for a different reason: she had a particularly sharp-edged face—brow and nose and chin had a honed look to them. The wife, who had more pleasing features, evoked respect and compassion. It was touching to see her sit on the edge of the empty cot beside her husband's and tuck in the hem of her skirt under her knees. She could not have been more than twenty, and already she wore the sadness of her widowhood. The glare of the naked electric bulb that hung from the ridgepole of the deck's canvas roof accentuated it, revealed that she was about six months gone with child, and called attention to her already full breasts, under a rust-colored *camisa,* that soon would be nourishing yet another life.

It was at Dias, four hours before, where the accident had occurred. Although Dias was a rich port, neither the government nor the local association of copra and rice merchants had provided it with a wharf. The old method of ferrying cargo by small outriggered *paraos* was less costly; perhaps, it was even thought to be picturesque. But loading was possible only in good weather. And already the noroeste had come. The same waves that pounded at the side of the *Adela* at anchor lashed at the frail paraos that were rowed over toward the ship and were brought into position for hauling up copra. The man, one of the *cargadores,* had fallen off the ship's side.

He would have gone to the bottom had he not let go of the copra sack that he had strained to hold aloft and had he not been caught across the hips by the outriggers of his parao. Nevertheless, the next wave that had lifted the ship and gathered strength from under her keel flung him head-long, it seemed, toward the prow of the boat. The blunt end of this dugout pressed his body against the black, tar-coated side of the *Adela.* Only with considerable difficulty was the crew able to get him clear, for the sea kept rising and falling and this caused the prow's head to scrape continuously against the ship's side. The crew had expected to find a mass of broken flesh and bones, but in actuality the man came through quite intact. He did not start moaning and writhing until his wet undershirt and shorts had been changed and he had been laid out on the cot. Something had broken or had burst open, somewhere inside him. There was nothing that could be done further for him, except to keep him on board.

His family was sent for. The wife, accompanied by her mother, clambered up the ship's side thirty minutes later, to the jocose shouts of "Now you can see San Roque!" from innocent well-wishers in the parao. The shippers, the Dias Development Co., had sent a telegram to the provincial doctor at San Roque, and an agent of the company came on board and personally committed the cargador to the care of the captain. When at last the fifty-ton copra shipment was on board, the *Adela* weighed anchor.

Now, his having transferred the man from the third-class to the first-class section earned the captain some praise, and the connection between this act and the pleasant change in the weather elicited much speculation. If only the man did not groan so pitifully; if only he kept his misery to himself; if

only the two women were less preoccupied, too, by some bitter and long-unresolved conflict between them. "Don't you
think he is hungry?" the mother once asked; to which the
wife answered, "He does not like food. You know that." And
then the mother asked, "How about water? He'll be thirsty,
perhaps." To which the wife's reply was, "I shall go below
deck and fetch some water." The matter could have stopped
there, but the mother wanted the last word. "That's better
than just standing or sitting around."

The wife got up and walked away, only to return about
ten minutes later with a pitcher and a drinking cup from the
mess room below. The mother had the pitcher and drinking
cup placed at the foot of the sick man's bed, for, as she explained, "He will ask for water any time and you won't be
near enough to help me." The mother waited to see what her
daughter would make of this; and the latter did have her say:
"I'll be right here, Mother, if that's all you're worried about."

The man grew restless. His wife's assurances (she said,
again and again, "You'll be all right!") drew nothing but interminable sighs ("O God of mine!"). Between the man and
his wife, some inexplicable source of irritation had begun to
fester. "It is when you try to move that the pain comes," the
wife chided him gently. "We are getting there soon. It will
not be long now." Whereupon the man managed to turn and
raise his knee under the blanket. The blanket made a hump
like one of the Maniwala mountains in the distance, and he
let out a moan, followed by, "But this boat is so very slow.
God of mine! Why can't we go faster? Let the captain make
the boat go faster. Tell him. Will someone go and tell him?"

Almost out of breath after this exertion, he lay still. The
mother, this time as if her son-in-law were an ally, took it
upon herself to comfort him. "Better keep quiet and don't
tire yourself. The captain will make the boat go faster,

surely." And by putting down his knee carefully, the hump, those high ranges of the Maniwala that the blanket had been made into, leveled off now into foothills.

The business of the telegram came after this lull. It was preceded by a prolonged groan, and then the question was right there before them: "And did they send the telegram?" "They," of course, meant the company in whose service the man had enlisted as cargador. If the answer to his question was in the affirmative, then there was reason to hope that the doctor would attend to him and put him together again and restore him to his work. His wife assured him that the telegram had been dispatched. "So you be quiet," she added. "These people here would not want to be disturbed now. They want to sleep." She looked about her, as if to solicit the approval of the twenty or twenty-five passengers around—which included merchants, students, and at least three public-school teachers on some Christmas holiday jaunt.

The mother asked about food—a proper question, although under the circumstances perhaps a tactless one. "Then I will go look for some food if you are that hungry, Mother," the daughter said. "But I don't care about food," the mother assured her. "And did I ever tell you that I wanted to eat?" Whereupon the daughter made a point of declaring that she was not hungry—"Let me tell you that, Mother." Then perhaps her most loving daughter, the mother said, was simply "too choosy about food, that's why. Go down below and ask for something to eat . . . whatever you can find." She added the solemn injunction, as if she had never believed her daughter's claim about not being hungry at all. "Don't worry about me, Mother," the wife added, pointedly. "I don't get hungry that easily." And then to round off this phase of their quarrel, the mother said, loud enough for anyone who cared to hear, "Maybe it's sitting at the captain's table that you've been waiting for all this time."

The daughter said nothing in reply and the mother did not press her advantage, either. It was clear, though, that the insinuation was not one easily dismissed. The mother had given thought to something out of the ordinary; the air, as Arenas put it, became rife with conjectures. It was not difficult to remember, he said, that, as a class, ship's officers, or sailors in general, are reluctant to regard women as beings endowed with the highest values. What particularly had to be understood, Arenas said, was why the mother thought of her daughter in some such awful connection as this.

Four hours later, after the *Adela* had docked at the San Roque pier and had begun discharging passengers and cargo, the subject came up again, Arenas said. Perhaps the first person to disembark had been the captain himself, to infer from the fact that somebody, possibly one of the mates, had been heard to call out to someone standing on the wharf: "Duty before pleasure, chief!" A Southern Star Navigation Co. jeep had pulled up the ramp and then hurried off the mile-long seaside road toward town, into San Roque *poblacion* itself. The town was brightly lighted, particularly the section along the water.

"Now he's gone and we have not even thanked him," said the mother. "And the doctor has not come. How can we leave this ship? Answer that one," she demanded. "You are too proud, that's what. A word or two of thanks was all that you needed to say, surely." The wife remained silent. "And he could have taken you along in the jeep, to fetch the doctor . . . if there was that telegram, and it has been received. . . ." She did not go further. The wife reminded the mother calmly that the telegram had been sent. "So what harm could it have done to have spoken to the captain, to have reminded him about the doctor, since he was riding into town anyway?" the mother said; and to this the daughter's reply, said Arenas, was a kind of serenity that can come only from knowledge, "All men know is to take advantage of us, Mother."

Taken aback by these words, the mother searched the faces of the people around her. The latter were crowding at the railing to watch the cargadores tossing pieces of boards from over the ship's side to the wharf ten feet away, with someone somewhere chanting: "A hundred and fifty-three . . . and fifty-four . . . and fifty-five . . . ," the wood collecting askew on the fast-mounting pile. Again, from their corral at the stern, there was heard the low of the cows blending afresh with the man's groans, the chanting of the numbers, and the clatter of the boards. The wife talked on softly: "We have arrived, and it's the doctor's jeep we're now waiting for . . . ," wiping her husband's brow with a handkerchief. "Two hundred and three . . . and four . . . and five . . ." the counter sang, from somewhere down below. "This is San Roque now," she continued. "It's a big town . . . oh the people!" Her husband sweated profusely. "And the lights are bright, and oh so many. Rest now, and tomorrow we can see the town," she said softly, folding her handkerchief this way and that, so as not to get any section of it too damp.

It was at this point, Arenas said, that from down the road came a sweep of headlights and the blare of a jeep's horn. The light caught the man who was chanting his count of the boards. He called out the numbers louder. The jeep pulled up in the middle of the now-cluttered wharf. What with the copra stacked, row upon row, and the lauan boards from San Tome scattered about, hardly was there space for the jeep. The driver could only go so far; he slid off his seat awkwardly and demanded of the man who had been doing the counting, "How much longer is this going to take?" And the other replied, "Possibly until two o'clock . . . what with the men we have. You know how it is, sir." To which the other said, sternly: "Stop calling me 'sir.' And to think that the captain just told me he'll put out in two hours, not a second later."

Words, Arenas said, which, although intended for someone prompted the wife to say to her husband: "They'll first move you over there, to the wharf . . . that will be solid ground at least . . ." She dropped her voice to a whisper, "There we shall wait for the doctor."

Across the ten feet of water between the ship's side and the dock, the ship's lights fell harshly on the piles and on the heads and arms of the cargadores who slid up and down the gangplank with copra sacks on their shoulders, looking like so many oversized ants. The driver had returned to his jeep, and, maneuvering, got stuck between the wall of copra to his left and another pile of lumber to his right. The man who had addressed him as "sir" stopped working to watch; so did the man who had been chanting the count. "What shamelessness!" cried the wife, when the jeep's light turned in the direction of the first-class section of the deck. The clatter of the boards had ceased. Up on the deck, the wife shouted: "What does he want of me? What does he want me to do now?" For the jeep's lights were too bright; she shielded her eyes with her arm but could not keep them from hurting. Too embarrassed over her daughter's behavior, the mother explained: "She's overwrought. Forgive her," she begged. "I don't know why it has come to this. Why must God punish us so?"

Once more the driver tried to maneuver his jeep, and all the time his lights seemed to fix themselves forever on the wife, who, to meet the challenge now, sprang away from the ship's railing and rushed down to the lower deck, shouting: "Here, here I am . . . Take me! What can you want of me?"

It was that way, Arenas said. Two hours later, the man was moved to the wharf and there, behind the sacks of copra and piles of lauan lumber, the wife and the mother waited. Word was abroad that the captain, who had returned from town, had said that he had contacted the doctor. Contacted, Arenas said.

That was the very word our Arenas used. And wasn't that so revealing! Did he want to remind us about the war, the same one during which the *Adela* had swept the mine-strewn sea in behalf of progress and civilization? We didn't know at first what he meant, beyond being certain that the word belonged to all time, and that, thus, he seemed to say: "All this because you must understand; you must forgive, even."

But we didn't want him to be apologetic like the mother-in-law he had described; and so, afterward, when he brought up the subject of the two women and the man, wearing that same worried look on his face with which we had become familiar, we had to urge him: "Better not think about it any more."

1954

The Whispering Woman

AS THEY STOOD IN THE STREETLIGHT, MR. FLORES'S face a notebook-paper buff in the full glare from the nearby lamppost, Mr. Malto caught the strange gleam in his friend's eyes.

"Won't you join me for supper?" he asked. The boarding house was only a few steps away.

"No, thanks," said Mr. Flores.

Mr. Malto thought of other inducements. He remembered the week's batch of the *Tribune* which had arrived in the mail.

"I've the Manila papers. Don't you want to see them?"

"Maybe, some other time," said Mr. Flores.

Mr. Malto felt defeated. Perhaps Flores wouldn't even consider rooming with him. It was a pity, he thought. One always lodged at Mrs. Bello's, but Flores was different. It was customary to spend one's afternoon at the Rex Bowling Alley, or the Evangeline Drugstore, but Flores preferred walking down the wharf and watching sailboats bring in copra from the islands across the bay. For his Mrs. Bello, Flores had an old couple on Calle Real in a tumbledown frame house.

"All right, if that's what you like," said Mr. Malto without resentment.

"See you tomorrow," said Mr. Flores.

Though his chuckle was heartening, it was final—like a period. Mr. Malto knew he would never get him. Too bad. And all the time, he thought, he was doing the fellow a favor.

Mr. Malto crossed the landing and hurried up the stairs, thinking: Well, anyway, I'm having the whole place to myself.

It had had its heyday, to judge from the picture album

on display at the *sala*. There all of them smiled tooth-
somely or laughed off the immediate threats that life posed to
them. Oh, you young clerks, schoolteachers, health inspec-
tors, bachelors all, who have somehow found your way here!
Mr. Malto felt like saying something unpleasant to everyone
of them.

There were three daughters, people at the Evangeline
Drugstore had said. And from the Rex Bowling Alley crowd,
Mr. Malto had learned other things: two of the girls had
found good husbands—Fe, a Public Works supervisor; Es-
peranza, a Weather Bureau man. Mr. Malto did not ask
any more whether the two men had been, even though but
briefly, Mrs. Bello's boarders. He felt he did not need to
know, having been assured that they had prospered in their
respective stations.

For Mrs. Bello, who now had only Charity to help her carry
on, a poor year loomed ahead. But it need not be a bad one;
she had Mr. Malto, at least. And Charity, the third and only
unmarried daughter, looked intelligent enough. Mr. Malto
felt he could count on being well fed and comfortable and,
perhaps, happy. It was sad to see that his friend Flores had
no such promise before him.

Supper tonight would be beef stew, rice, and two bananas.
There was a surprise item, mackerel in rich, sweet-sour
sauce. Charity served, while her mother got Mr. Malto
posted on the gossip of the day.

"What . . . a soldier? Killed himself?" Mr. Malto asked.

Neither at the Evangeline Drugstore nor at the Rex Bowling Alley had Mr. Malto heard about it, strangely enough.

Mrs. Bello had all the details. The poor fellow had put the
muzzle of his gun in his mouth and then pulled the trigger
with his big toe.

"Woman trouble, maybe," Mr. Malto said.

"Rice, sir?" Charity said, offering him the bowl.

He took only a small portion. He was deeply troubled by the suicide. Was the gun the only remedy? Could it not have been avoided? Could there have been some other way? Mrs. Bello's word for the soldier's trouble was cowardice: Mr. Malto heard her say it clearly.

"Fish, sir?" said Charity. She pushed the sweet-sour dish closer to him, crinkling the tablecloth and smoothing it carefully afterwards so that its flowers, red and yellow, nameless roses of the factory, seemed less unreal. "Mother taught me how to make this," she volunteered.

"Oh, it's nice," Mr. Malto said, without conviction.

Mrs. Bello, who had taken the seat to his right, seemed almost to spill over; for besides being quite fat, she was earnest about resuming her story and, as was so characteristically her style, she had to lean all the way. She could not carry on a conversation otherwise; some defect in her throat made it impossible. Instead of talking, she whispered.

"Beg your pardon?" Mr. Malto said politely.

The bumble of a bee? The whiz of a wasp, perhaps? He realized there was no sound which Mrs. Bello's whisper resembled.

Sometimes Mrs. Bello put her lips too close to his ear, and a tingle would run up his spine. Throwing her head back later, she might chuckle pleasantly. Then he would say "Oh," as if he had understood her when, in fact, he had only as graciously suffered as he could the interminable babble it had been.

Well, he would just have to get used to it, he said to himself, retiring to his favorite rocking chair in the sala while mother and daughter, following some self-imposed rule of their trade, hied away to the kitchen to eat their supper. But there was something different tonight. It seemed that, as he lighted a cigarette, the scratching of his matchstick started up the clatter of their forks and spoons. His first puff recalled to Mr. Malto the soothing quiet of this very same hour of the evening before. Up the window, to his left, muggy air welled out from the street.

The shell-paned shutters offered a plaque of sky glittering with stars. He knew from this that it would be a warm night—rather the kind you might sit up through enjoyably, given the right company and some lively topic for conversation.

Had he succeeded in getting Mr. Flores up for supper, they'd be discussing the Hare-Hawes-Cutting Bill. By and large, Buenavista belonged to that camp. Mr. Malto thought that he, personally, belonged to another; he stood for a more righteous kind of nationalism. The politicians, so far, had not quite organized the party he might join. Now, alone, he could only rock his heavy supper away. He smoked with a joyous respect for his package of Piedmont.

Already, Mrs. Bello and Charity were through, it seemed, with their meal. He recalled the dead soldier, but rather than listen to Mrs. Bello, Mr. Malto thought, he should be out there in his room, working.

He could hear them moving about the kitchen, and once again mother and daughter impinged on his thoughts. They'd perhaps join him under the buzzing Coleman lamp one evening—who could tell? Once he had managed to carry on a conversation with Charity. She had looked all of her eighteen years, the last two spent, as he well knew, at a Manila dressmaking school. She had sat there, mildly handsome, across the table from him, with the embroidered runner and the flower vase between them; and he had said:

"When will you be opening that dress shop?"

"It'll be up to Mother."

Thus, all over the country, Mr. Malto thought, on some such Sunday evening as this, ineffectual young men were visiting similarly ineffectual young girls and bogging down in a similar mire of dialog.

It could look, though, as if he were one of the young men who paid her some attention, which in fact he had not even thought of doing. Meanwhile, moths nettled the lamp, some falling dead on his hair and others on the embroidered tablerunner. Quite simply a ghastly thing, especially with Mrs. Bello there, edging over to whisper again—something in his ear . . .

Rather than risk all that now, he hurried away to his room. The dining table stood directly in the way. It was a bother having to turn all around. As if frantic about something, he reached for the door jamb.

His room looked as good as on that day he had brought in his suitcase two weeks ago. He had had, then, to try the iron bed. He had found it springy enough; up till now it had not begun to creak. He changed into his pajamas, thinking how things around here had not been so bad, really. The food had been good, and his room was fine, anyway you looked at it. Flores—how could he possibly be better lodged and fed? It would be no use trying to get him to live out here, though. Let him alone . . .

Mr. Malto's work—three pages that must be filled out with plans for the week's Civics and History classes—awaited him at the desk by his bed. But as he buckled down to the task, adjusting the wick of the table lamp so that the light became agreeably brighter, Mrs. Bello's favorite little stories, which had been whispered into his ear through several delightful meals, came back to him.

She had been full of them. Strange macabre accounts of

illnesses and deaths, of middle-aged men stiffening up in their beds with strangers standing by, glassy-eyed in their unconcern. She had told them about lonely Chinese shop-keepers doped up in their dens; about drunks hitting each other with bottles and, their skulls cracked, babbling away some woman's name on their lips. And they were one and the same story, however varied they appeared.

Not only did Mrs. Bello tell them in the one manner she knew, but she weighted them with the same message. To Mr. Malto it was something at once fascinating and dreadful. He felt that they made his thinking wander in the direction of a hell or purgatory. A sense of destiny seemed to hang on every word Mrs. Bello breathed. Somehow, too, her stories mixed readily with what he, as a teacher, knew—about wars and revolutions, the murder of kings and presidents of re-publics, the fall of governments. The thought cut a groove in his mind. He gasped for air but only breathed in the mugginess that rose from the street below.

He had to put his work away. He extinguished the lamp. The house was quiet. No, there were light footsteps outside, followed by the faint clatter of glass. It had become a famil-iar sound these past three nights. Only he had not bothered about it. He had often heard his heart thumping, too. Those footsteps had stopped just outside his door, and he had never gone out to investigate. He did not wish to now. It was time for taps; the bugle call would come all the way from across town. He did not want to miss it.

The constabulary barracks was down over to the south, and the night wind now played tricks with the bugle. It carried the soul-freighted notes over the rooftops and flung them against the wall of coconut-covered hills. The notes re-bounded in broken echoes. Then, again over the rooftops the fragments gathered and merged into a great cry of loneliness.

It confirmed to Mr. Malto the death of the soldier. Truth was in every shred of Mrs. Bello's whispers.

She had fixed his bed with fresh sheets, and the pillow now under his head was as soft as the agar-agar bars he had played with as a boy in his mother's kitchen. More thoughtful than his mother had ever been, Mrs. Bello had provided him with a second pillow, an *abrasador* for his legs. He had not quite appreciated the gift before. Now it surprised him that the dutch pillow was as ample as life; he could have convinced himself that it was warm, that in reality it was flesh.

He tossed about restlessly, willing enough to admit that he had debased his thoughts. So this was what it all would lead to—marriage. Who wanted to marry whom? Mrs. Bello? Charity? So this was why Mrs. Bello had encouraged him to give out little confidences about himself. Nine years in the government service and with a little something tucked away in the Postal Savings Bank. He really had no cares in this world, nor perhaps in the next. And in return she had told him about her dear dead, the husband who, living, had been a constabulary sergeant—and a clean man. Although he had captured a bandit, rounded up opium smokers, and caught fishermen with sticks of dynamite in their hands, Sergeant Bello had died in bed. To Mrs. Bello, this was proof enough of grace. Remarry? No, it would spoil things. And she shook her head—her whole whispering body, even. It seemed to Mr. Malto, wiping now the moist feel off his ears, that he could see her fat rippling loose all over her.

He rubbed his ear against the starch-smooth pillow cover, as if to drive off every single sensation which, together, summoned up all the things Mrs. Bello had told him. He tried to sleep. His legs jerked off the abrasador, and then he fell into the abyss between sleep and waking, and he thought of coffins walking on two short legs, carrying suitcases and look-

ing for fat, smiling landladies, calling, "Flores! Flores!"—
although in the end it was he, Malto, who answered.

He got up in a cold sweat and struck a match. The light
was slow in coming. The lamp had a big, round oil container; and this caught the glow and became a concave mirror
that tossed back at him a contorted face. He hardly recognized the bleary eyes and the wet-looking nose. It was as if
he had mourned the dead soldier, mourned the lost men,
and mourned the wanderers who had always so little time to
indulge in their dreams, having been caught by some grim
hand—that might also be the big toe—before the moment
came when they themselves had to be borne away.

His fear resolved itself into thirst. "A glass of water . . .
water!" he cried, silently but trustfully—to throw off the
morbidity, to test himself as quite awake.

He must blame it all on his heavy dinner and the muggy
air. As he opened the door, something gleamed in the room;
it was as if through those shell-paned window shutters, near
where he had sat earlier, some tokens of sifted starlight had
fallen.

It was a pitcher of water. A drinking glass stood beside
it. There was a catch in his throat when he picked up the
glass. The water he poured had that gleam he had caught in
Flores's eyes.

"Thank you, Charity," he said, softly, to the dark. "Good-
night."

1955

The Bread of Salt

USUALLY I WAS IN BED BY TEN AND UP BY FIVE and thus was ready for one more day of my fourteenth year. Unless Grandmother had forgotten, the fifteen centavos for the baker down Progreso Street—and how I enjoyed jingling those coins in my pocket!—would be in the empty fruit jar in the cupboard. I would remember then that rolls were what Grandmother wanted because recently she had lost three molars. For young people like my cousins and myself, she had always said that the kind called *pan de sal* ought to be quite all right.

The bread of salt! How did it get that name? From where did its flavor come, through what secret action of flour and yeast? At the risk of being jostled from the counter by early buyers, I would push my way into the shop so that I might watch the men who, stripped to the waist, worked their long flat wooden spades in and out of the glowing maw of the oven. Why did the bread come nut-brown and the size of my little fist? And why did it have a pair of lips convulsed into a painful frown? In the half light of the street, and hurrying, the paper bag pressed to my chest, I felt my curiosity a little gratified by the oven-fresh warmth of the bread I was proudly bringing home for breakfast.

Well I knew how Grandmother would not mind if I nibbled away at one piece; perhaps, I might even eat two, to be charged later against my share at the table. But that would be betraying a trust; and so, indeed, I kept my purchase intact. To guard it from harm, I watched my steps and avoided the dark street corners.

For my reward, I had only to look in the direction of the

sea wall and the fifty yards or so of riverbed beyond it, where
an old Spaniard's house stood. At low tide, when the bed was
dry and the rocks glinted with broken bottles, the stone fence
of the Spaniard's compound set off the house as if it were a
castle. Sunrise brought a wash of silver upon the roofs of the
laundry and garden sheds which had been built low and close
to the fence. On dull mornings the light dripped from the
bamboo screen which covered the veranda and hung some
four or five yards from the ground. Unless it was August,
when the damp, northeast monsoon had to be kept away
from the rooms, three servants raised the screen promptly at
six-thirty until it was completely hidden under the veranda
eaves. From the sound of the pulleys, I knew it was time to
set out for school.

It was in his service, as a coconut plantation overseer, that
Grandfather had spent the last thirty years of his life. Grandmother had been widowed three years now. I often wondered
whether I was being depended upon to spend the years ahead
in the service of this great house. One day I learned that
Aida, a classmate in high school, was the old Spaniard's
niece. All my doubts disappeared. It was as if, before his
death, Grandfather had spoken to me about her, concealing
the seriousness of the matter by putting it over as a joke. If
now I kept true to the virtues, she would step out of her bedroom ostensibly to say Good Morning to her uncle. Her real
purpose, I knew, was to reveal thus her assent to my desire.

On quiet mornings I imagined the patter of her shoes upon
the wooden veranda floor as a further sign, and I would hurry
off to school, taking the route she had fixed for me past the
post office, the town plaza and the church, the health center east of the plaza, and at last the school grounds. I asked
myself whether I would try to walk with her and decided it
would be the height of rudeness. Enough that in her blue

skirt and white middy she would be half a block ahead and, from that distance, perhaps throw a glance in my direction, to bestow upon my heart a deserved and abundant blessing. I believed it was but right that, in some such way as this, her mission in my life was disguised.

Her name, I was to learn many years later, was a convenient mnemonic for the qualities to which argument might aspire. But in those days it was a living voice. "Oh that you might be worthy of uttering me," it said. And how I endeavored to build my body so that I might live long to honor her. With every victory at singles at the handball court— the game was then the craze at school—I could feel my body glow in the sun as though it had instantly been cast in bronze. I guarded my mind and did not let my wits go astray. In class I would not allow a lesson to pass unmastered. Our English teacher could put no question before us that did not have a ready answer in my head. One day he read Robert Louis Stevenson's *The Sire de Maletroit's Door*, and we were so enthralled that our breaths trembled. I knew then that somewhere, sometime in the not too improbable future, a benign old man with a lantern in his hand would also detain me in a secret room, and there daybreak would find me thrilled by the sudden certainty that I had won Aida's hand.

It was perhaps on my violin that her name wrought such a tender spell. Maestro Antonino remarked the dexterity of my stubby fingers. Quickly I raced through Alard—until I had all but committed two thirds of the book to memory. My short, brown arm learned at last to draw the bow with grace. Sometimes, when practising my scales in the early evening, I wondered if the sea wind carrying the straggling notes across the pebbled river did not transform them into Schubert's "Serenade."

At last Mr. Custodio, who was in charge of our school

orchestra, became aware of my progress. He moved me from second to first violin. During the Thanksgiving Day program he bade me render a number, complete with pizzicati and harmonics.

"Another Vallejo! Our own Albert Spalding!" I heard from the front row.

Aida, I thought, would be in the audience. I looked around quickly but could not see her. As I retired to my place in the orchestra I heard Pete Saez, the trombone player, call my name.

"You must join *my* band," he said. "Look, we'll have many engagements soon. It'll be vacation time."

Pete pressed my arm. He had for some time now been asking me to join the Minviluz Orchestra, his private band. All I had been able to tell him was that I had my schoolwork to mind. He was twenty-two. I was perhaps too young to be going around with him. He earned his school fees and supported his mother hiring out his band at least three or four times a month. He now said:

"Tomorrow we play at the funeral of a Chinese—four to six in the afternoon; in the evening, Judge Roldan's silver wedding anniversary; Sunday, the municipal dance."

My head began to whirl. On the stage, in front of us, the principal had begun a speech about America. Nothing he could say seemed interesting. I thought of the money I would earn. For several days now I had but one wish, to buy a box of linen stationery. At night when the house was quiet I would fill the sheets with words that would tell Aida how much I adored her. One of these mornings, perhaps before school closed for the holidays, I would borrow her algebra book and there, upon a good pageful of equations, there I would slip my message, tenderly pressing the leaves of the book. She would perhaps never write back. Neither by post nor by hand would a reply reach me. But no matter; it would be a silence full of voices.

That night I dreamed I had returned from a tour of the world's music centers; the newspapers of Manila had been generous with praise. I saw my picture on the cover of a magazine. A writer had described how, many years ago, I used to trudge the streets of Buenavista with my violin in a battered black cardboard case. In New York, he reported, a millionaire had offered me a Stradivarius violin, with a card that bore the inscription: "In admiration of a genius your own people must surely be proud of." I dreamed I spent a weekend at the millionaire's country house by the Hudson. A young girl in a blue skirt and white middy clapped her lily-white hands and, her voice trembling, cried "Bravo!"

What people now observed at home was the diligence with which I attended to my violin lessons. My aunt, who had come from the farm to join her children for the holidays, brought with her a maidservant, and to the poor girl was given the chore of taking the money to the baker's for rolls and pan de sal. I realized at once that it would be no longer becoming on my part to make these morning trips to the baker's. I could not thank my aunt enough.

I began to chafe on being given other errands. Suspecting my violin to be the excuse, my aunt remarked:

"What do you want to be a musician for? At parties, musicians always eat last."

Perhaps, I said to myself, she was thinking of a pack of dogs scrambling for scraps tossed over the fence by some careless kitchen maid. She was the sort you could depend on to say such vulgar things. For that reason, I thought, she ought not to be taken seriously at all.

But the remark hurt me. Although Grandmother had

counseled me kindly to mind my work at school, I went again and again to Pete Saez's house for rehearsals.

She had demanded that I deposit with her my earnings; I had felt too weak to refuse. Secretly, I counted the money and decided not to ask for it until I had enough with which to buy a brooch. Why this time I wanted to give Aida a brooch, I didn't know. But I had set my heart on it. I searched the downtown shops. The Chinese clerks, seeing me so young, were annoyed when I inquired about prices.

At last the Christmas season began. I had not counted on Aida's leaving home, and remembering that her parents lived in Badajoz, my torment was almost unbearable. Not once had I tried to tell her of my love. My letters had remained unwritten, and the algebra book unborrowed. There was still the brooch to find, but I could not decide on the sort of brooch I really wanted. And the money, in any case, was in Grandmother's purse, which smelled of "Tiger Balm." I grew somewhat feverish as our class Christmas program drew near. Finally it came; it was a warm December afternoon. I decided to leave the room when our English teacher announced that members of the class might exchange gifts. I felt fortunate; Pete was at the door, beckoning to me. We walked out to the porch where, Pete said, he would tell me a secret.

It was about an *asalto* the next Sunday which the Buenavista Women's Club wished to give Don Esteban's daughters, Josefina and Alicia, who were arriving on the morning steamer from Manila. The spinsters were much loved by the ladies. Years ago, when they were younger, these ladies studied solfeggio with Josefina and the piano and harp with Alicia. As Pete told me all this, his lips ash-gray from practising all morning on his trombone, I saw in my mind the sisters in their silk dresses, shuffling off to church for the

evening benediction. They were very devout, and the Buenavista ladies admired that. I had almost forgotten that they
were twins and, despite their age, often dressed alike. In
low-bosomed voile bodices and white summer hats, I remembered, the pair had attended Grandfather's funeral, at
old Don Esteban's behest. I wondered how successful they
had been in Manila during the past three years in the matter
of finding suitable husbands.

"This party will be a complete surprise," Pete said, looking around the porch as if to swear me to secrecy. "They've
hired our band."

I joined my classmates in the room, greeting everyone
with a Merry Christmas jollier than that of the others. When
I saw Aida in one corner unwrapping something two girls
had given her, I found the boldness to greet her also.

"Merry Christmas," I said in English, as a hairbrush and
a powder case emerged from the fancy wrapping. It seemed
to me rather apt that such gifts went to her. Already several girls were gathered around Aida. Their eyes glowed with
envy, it seemed to me, for those fair cheeks and the bobbed
dark-brown hair which lineage had denied them.

I was too dumbstruck by my own meanness to hear exactly
what Aida said in answer to my greeting. But I recovered
shortly and asked:

"Will you be away during the vacation?"

"No, I'll be staying here," she said. When she added that
her cousins were arriving and that a big party in their honor
was being planned, I remarked:

"So you know all about it?" I felt I had to explain that the
party was meant to be a surprise, an asalto.

And now it would be nothing of the kind, really. The
women's club matrons would hustle about, disguising their
scurrying around for cakes and candies as for some baptis-

mal party or other. In the end, the Rivas sisters would outdo them. Boxes of meringues, bonbons, ladyfingers, and cinnamon buns that only the Swiss bakers in Manila could make were perhaps coming on the boat with them. I imagined a table glimmering with long-stemmed punch glasses; enthroned in that array would be a huge brick-red bowl of gleaming china with golden flowers around the brim. The local matrons, however hard they tried, however sincere their efforts, were bound to fail in their aspiration to rise to the level of Don Esteban's daughters. Perhaps, I thought, Aida knew all this. And that I should share in a foreknowledge of the matrons' hopes was a matter beyond love. Aida and I could laugh together with the gods.

At seven, on the appointed evening, our small band gathered quietly at the gate of Don Esteban's house, and when the ladies arrived in their heavy shawls and trim *panuelos,* twittering with excitement, we were commanded to play the *Poet and Peasant* overture. As Pete directed the band, his eyes glowed with pride for his having been part of the big event. The multicolored lights that the old Spaniard's gardeners had strung along the vine-covered fence were switched on, and the women remarked that Don Esteban's daughters might have made some preparations after all. Pete hid his face from the glare. If the women felt let down, they did not show it.

The overture shuffled along to its climax while five men in white shirts bore huge boxes of goods into the house. I recognized one of the bakers in spite of the uniform. A chorus of confused greetings, and the women trooped into the house; and before we had settled in the *sala* to play "A Basket of Roses," the heavy damask curtains at the far end of the room were drawn and a long table richly spread was revealed under the chandeliers. I remembered that, in our haste to be on hand for the asalto, Pete and I had discouraged the members of the band from taking their suppers.

"You've done us a great honor!" Josefina, the more buxom of the twins, greeted the ladies.

"Oh, but you have not allowed us to take you by surprise!" the ladies demurred in a chorus.

There were sighs and further protestations amid a rustle of skirts and the glitter of earrings. I saw Aida in a long, flowing white gown and wearing an arch of *sampaguita* flowers on her hair. At her command, two servants brought out a gleaming harp from the music room. Only the slightest scraping could be heard because the servants were barefoot. As Aida directed them to place the instrument near the seats we occupied, my heart leaped to my throat. Soon she was lost among the guests, and we played "The Dance of the Glowworms." I kept my eyes closed and held for as long as I could her radiant figure before me.

Alicia played on the harp and then, in answer to the deafening applause, she offered an encore. Josefina sang afterward. Her voice, though a little husky, fetched enormous sighs. For her encore, she gave "The Last Rose of Summer"; and the song brought back snatches of the years gone by. Memories of solfeggio lessons eddied about us, as if there were rustling leaves scattered all over the hall. Don Esteban appeared. Earlier, he had greeted the crowd handsomely, twisting his mustache to hide a natural shyness before talkative women. He stayed long enough to listen to the harp again, whispering in his rapture: "Heavenly. Heavenly . . ."

By midnight, the merrymaking lagged. We played while the party gathered around the great table at the end of the sala. My mind traveled across the seas to the distant cities I had dreamed about. The sisters sailed among the ladies like two great white liners amid a fleet of tugboats in a bay. Someone had thoughtfully remembered—and at last Pete Saez signaled to us to put our instruments away. We walked in single file across the hall, led by one of the barefoot servants.

Behind us a couple of hoarse sopranos sang "La Paloma" to the accompaniment of the harp, but I did not care to find out who they were. The sight of so much silver and china confused me. There was more food before us than I had ever imagined. I searched in my mind for the names of the dishes; but my ignorance appalled me. I wondered what had happened to the boxes of food that the Buenavista ladies had sent up earlier. In a silver bowl was something, I discovered, that appeared like whole egg yolks that had been dipped in honey and peppermint. The seven of us in the orchestra were all of one mind about the feast; and so, confident that I was with friends, I allowed my covetousness to have its sway and not only stuffed my mouth with this and that confection but also wrapped up a quantity of those egg-yolk things in several sheets of napkin paper. None of my companions had thought of doing the same, and it was with some pride that I slipped the packet under my shirt. There, I knew, it would not bulge.

"Have you eaten?"

I turned around. It was Aida. My bow tie seemed to tighten around my collar. I mumbled something, I did not know what.

"If you wait a little while till they've gone, I'll wrap up a big package for you," she added.

I brought a handkerchief to my mouth. I might have honored her solicitude adequately and even relieved myself of any embarrassment; I could not quite believe that she had seen me, and yet I was sure that she knew what I had done, and I felt all ardor for her gone from me entirely.

I walked away to the nearest door, praying that the damask curtains might hide me in my shame. The door gave on to the veranda, where once my love had trod on sunbeams. Outside it was dark, and a faint wind was singing in the harbor.

With the napkin balled up in my hand, I flung out my arm to scatter the egg-yolk things in the dark. I waited for the soft sound of their fall on the garden-shed roof. Instead, I heard a spatter in the rising night-tide beyond the stone fence. Farther away glimmered the light from Grandmother's window, calling me home.

But the party broke up at one or thereabouts. We walked away with our instruments after the matrons were done with their interminable good-byes. Then, to the tune of "Joy to the World," we pulled the Progreso Street shopkeepers out of their beds. The Chinese merchants were especially generous. When Pete divided our collection under a street lamp, there was already a little glow of daybreak.

He walked with me part of the way home. We stopped at the baker's when I told him that I wanted to buy with my own money some bread to eat on the way to Grandmother's house at the edge of the sea wall. He laughed, thinking it strange that I should be hungry. We found ourselves alone at the counter; and we watched the bakery assistants at work until our bodies grew warm from the oven across the door. It was not quite five, and the bread was not yet ready.

1958

On the Ferry

THEY HAD HAD MORE THAN ENOUGH OF IT DURING the two-and-a-half hour ride from Manila to the Batangas wharf. No seats had been available except those over at the rear of the bus, which was the part called "Hollywood." It used to be known as "The Kitchen" and, to say the least, it was hardly comfortable there. But some things just couldn't be helped—like getting to the bus station late, or being unable to keep your son in school. You had to accept all that—well, like "Hollywood."

Except for the bus seats, Mr. Lopez had run through these things before. Now in the comparative comfort of the ferry, he could run through them again. But he didn't care to, and, hoping he could cast them out of his mind, he turned to Nilo.

"Have you checked our luggage?"

The thin, bespectacled boy who sat on the wooden bench beside him replied, "Yes, Pa."

"Check again, please," Mr. Lopez said.

The boy got up and peeked under his seat where the *cargador* had pushed in an old suitcase, two boxes of books and magazines, and two grocery paper bags—their *pasalubong,* their homecoming presents.

It was almost sailing time. During the quarter of an hour that they had been on board—"Pa, let's avoid the rush," Nilo had suggested—a steady stream of people from Manila had arrived, like them, on passenger trucks that had raced through the heat and dust. Mr. Lopez had his son occupy one of the starboard benches, hoping that they could have it all to themselves. But presently a big party—three elderly ladies and two young girls—joined them, taking the other end of the bench. Tangerine-shirted cargadores followed after the ladies, piling up right in front of them baskets of fruit, suitcases, and groceries in paper bags, too—in the end, shoving these conveniently under the seat. One of the ladies took possession of the spot beside Nilo; and the two others, the far end of the bench, the two young girls between them. The latter were plain-looking and dressed in the St. Bridget's College uniform; they were perhaps spending the weekend with relatives in Calapan.

Mr. Lopez, who had been assistant district engineer in his day, had hoped he would not run into any acquaintances from Calapan. That he did not know who the women were pleased him. He was afraid he would only embarrass himself in the presence of former associates in the government service, or even mere business friends. The firm Lopez & Co., Builders, had won many a public works bid in its time and had constructed bridges and river control projects all over Mindoro. But what people would remember, Mr. Lopez feared, was the Bajao Dam. If foreign-owned timber concessions had denuded, through indiscriminate cutting, the once heavily forested country around Mt. Halcon, nobody would instantly see where the dam came into the picture. But the fact of the matter was that the big flood of December 1956 did wash it away. Contracts had since been difficult to come by.

The cargadores had stopped running up and down the deck. A shudder shook the entire length of the ferry; a whistle sounded, and the boat edged out of the wharf and turned toward the open sea.

It was a clear day, unusual for early July. Although Mr. Lopez had made the trip many times before, it had never quite ceased to fascinate him. Today Batangas receded slowly in the mid-morning sun, the dome of the old church and that of the provincial capitol flashing like twin gems of a pendant in its original box of green suede that had been snapped open, the hand trembling for joy.

As the ferry headed toward the Mindoro coast, the view from Mr. Lopez's side of the deck was obstructed by gray canvas awnings rudely flapping in the breeze. He found himself soon crossing over to the larboard, leaning on the rail. Hardly eighteen years ago, as a young engineer, he had married a girl from St. Bridget's; and it was on a ferry such as this one that the two of them had crossed over to Mindoro. He could not remember, though, whether the two of them had stood at the railings together, their future literally before them, and let some fragment of the Batangas skyline share as well their daydreaming.

Nilo had remained on the bench and had pulled out a magazine from somewhere. The bookworm, Mr. Lopez thought, as he returned to his seat, picking his way through the scattered baggage along the deck. The boy had his mother's forehead and chin; he was delicately built. The eyeglasses added two or three years to his sixteen, but he was very much a boy still. A year away from school—hoping his luck improved, Mr. Lopez told himself—Nilo would be ready for the heavier work of a sophomore engineering student. A sudden recollection of the boy's letters the year before, in which he had described how he had scrimped on food, sometimes limiting himself to a bottle of Coke for breakfast, touched in Mr. Lopez something tender and deep. The appalling fact that Lopez & Co., Builders, had been an utter failure moved him to pity for the boy, for this full year he would lose, for his having gotten himself a bankrupt father.

But Mr. Lopez caught himself, as it were; and, remarking on the magazine that Nilo was reading, he said: "Must be interesting!" He tried to sound cheerful. "What's it? A *Reader's Digest?*"

"It's their copy," Nilo said, pointing to the two St. Bridget girls. He turned the magazine around to allow his father a glimpse of the article he was reading, "My Most Unforgettable Character."

"Who's it about?" he asked.

"Go . . . e . . . thals," Nilo said. "He built the Panama Canal." He turned to the two girls and asked, "Isn't that how you pronounce it?"

"Go . . . thals!" the girls corrected him.

They were surprisingly outgoing, and there was no avoiding introductions now. Mr. Lopez chided his son lightly, "Keeping your friends all to yourself, eh?"

The two young girls called themselves Mary and Rose. The three elderly ladies were aunts of theirs, and the amazing thing was they were all called Miss Adeva and were elementary school teachers.

"Ah," said one Miss Adeva. "What they demand of us nowadays that science is very much in the air!"

"But we have no vocabulary for science in the national language," the second Miss Adeva protested. She was obviously a Tagalog teacher.

"Hmm. Isn't it true that you have to be good at math these days?" asked the third Miss Adeva, apparently the most innocent of the three.

"I don't know much about these things," Mr. Lopez demurred. "I am only a businessman now."

"You're being very modest, Engineer," said the first Miss Adeva.

The three ladies were a complete surprise. Judging by their appearance, Mr. Lopez could not have guessed they were abreast with the times and were troubled in their own way by some idea of progress. It was all very heartening.

"Look, Nilo," Mr. Lopez said to his son. "There's a canteen at the other end of the boat. Why don't you run over and get some soft drinks?"

The ladies begged him not to bother. The second Miss Adeva tugged at Nilo's sleeve, urging the boy not to leave his seat.

Meanwhile, Nilo had returned the magazine to the girl called Rose; and, pushing his eyeglasses up the bridge of his nose, he stood up and brought out the coins in his pocket. He counted them unembarrassedly, and the two St. Bridget girls were unable to hide their amusement.

"You have enough money there, haven't you?" Mr. Lopez asked, ready to offer Nilo a peso of his own.

"It's all right, Pa," the boy said.

"He's such a kid, really," said Mr. Lopez after Nilo had left them. "You go wrong these days, though, if you provide boys with too much pocket money."

"There's a wise father," said the first Miss Adeva.

To merit the remark, Mr. Lopez told the ladies what he felt they needed to know about Nilo. He was an engineering student at the University of the Philippines. "The highest standards, you know," he couldn't help adding.

On discovering that the ladies were very enthusiastic about engineering and that the profession was, in their view, becoming deservedly popular, Mr. Lopez realized he had to say something similarly apposite.

"A wise choice for Nilo," the second Miss Adeva said with conviction.

"Oh, you school people!" Mr. Lopez said, still casting about. "Well, you've certainly begun to produce a new type of student these days!"

"Thank you, thank you!" the second Miss Adeva said, flattered by the remark.

The third Miss Adeva declared that times had changed; for one thing, education had become too costly.

"Don't I know!" said Mr. Lopez. This was a subject about which he had a direct and personal knowledge, indeed. "And I, with only one college student in the family as yet . . ."

"How many do you expect to have?" the second Miss Adeva asked. "Don't tell us if it will embarrass you . . ."

"It's nothing to be secretive about, let me assure you, ladies," Mr. Lopez said. "I've three boys, and a little daughter."

"That's all?" said the third Miss Adeva, skeptically.

"Oh, more will be coming, of course," said the first Miss Adeva.

Mr. Lopez whispered something to her, and lest the two other should feel left out, he said, "What I said was merely that Mrs. Lopez is in the family way."

He was surprised hearing his own words. One more moment and he could have told the ladies the whole story of his life. But he checked this access of familiarity, judiciously limiting himself to his son's school career.

"He's his mother's favorite," Mr. Lopez said. He told them about Nilo's health, which had always been delicate; and he described his interview with the dean of the engineering college, who had given him a cigar and remarked: "Health's wealth, as well we know, Mr. Lopez," tapping him on the shoulder.

The ladies warmed up to the new subject. They were certain that living conditions in Manila were not particularly wholesome for young people. They complained about the dust and the noise, the crowded boardinghouses, and the jam-packed movie houses. All these must have contributed to Nilo's poor health, they decided, and Mr. Lopez whole-heartedly agreed.

"But where else can we send our boys these days?" he added, in the tone of one used to generous doses of compassion.

The question made the ladies sad. The first Miss Adeva, in particular, flicked her long eyelashes. "In any case," she said, "a boy such as yours . . . why, Mr. Lopez, you really ought not to work him too hard."

"That's what his mother always says," Mr. Lopez replied.

"And you must watch out," warned the second Miss Adeva. "Boys his age easily get pleurisy or something like that. I had a nephew, you know."

And they were discussing this luckless nephew when Nilo returned with seven bottles of Coke clasped together precariously, the straws already stuck into them. The deck heaved under his feet, the bench slid forward. It was all he could do to deliver the bottles safely.

As the ladies sipped their Cokes quietly, Mr. Lopez revealed that Nilo's mother had studied at St. Bridget's. But while this proved to be interesting in itself, especially to the two young ones, Mary and Rose—who asked Mr. Lopez: "Did Mrs. Lopez wear a uniform different from ours?"—the Adeva ladies returned to the problem of Nilo's health, expressing their great concern unequivocally. It was as if Nilo's return from the ship's canteen with the bottles of Coke awoke in them feelings that had long been dormant. He ought never to prefer his studies to his health; no, Nilo shouldn't, they said. The college was right in sending him home for a while. The first Miss Adeva said, addressing Nilo directly:

"You're only sixteen, as your father says." It was neither a question nor a statement of fact—to judge by the tone this particular Miss Adeva used. Before the boy—who looked quite puzzled—could say anything for himself, Mr. Lopez clarified the issue concerning his son's age: "Next September, to be exact."

Now Nilo was blushing from being made too much of, and perhaps because Mary and Rose were blushing, too. Still on the matter of age, the first Miss Adeva revealed her nieces were both sixteen also.

"They're twins, you see," she said, as if to explain whatever it was that might be thought of as inexplicable about youth.

The ferry was running into some rough sea, which meant that they had reached the middle of Verde Island Passage. For a good half hour, until the ferry came directly in the shelter of the island, it ran into three-foot waves that occasionally caused the benches to slip again or tilt back against the railings. The Adevas were wonderful sailors, so used they were to crossing the Passage. It was Nilo who looked every inch the poor sailor. Attentively, the first Miss Adeva, who had taken it upon herself to look after him, bade the seasick boy rest his head on the bench, giving him all the room he needed.

"He'll be all right," Mr. Lopez said. "Don't be bothered with him."

"In fifteen years or so—oh, who knows?" said the second Miss Adeva, dreamily. "There'll be a tunnel through here. We'll all be going by train."

"That's one reason we'll be needing more engineers," the third Miss Adeva said.

Now Nilo raised his head off the back of the bench, as if surprised to hear someone speak so confidently about the future. The sea had become smooth again. The sound of falling rain ran through the length of the ferry—a school of tuna, Mr. Lopez saw, was caught unawares in the path of the ship. An island, one of three that girded Calapan harbor, swung forward and the twins cried out:

"A boat!"

Mr. Lopez turned quickly to landward, and there it was: a five-ton *lanchon,* a one-masted sailboat, listing precipitously where the small island rose from a sheet of white sand into the thick underbrush fringed with coconuts.

The Adevas were excited and exchanged all sorts of conjectures, their breaths quivering. One said a leak had sprung, causing the boat to head for safety. The second Miss Adeva said that it sat on a rock right there. It didn't seem to move. The third Miss Adeva declared she could see no signs of a crew. The lanchon had been abandoned. Mr. Lopez wished that the ferry could get closer, although he knew that would be something of an impertinence.

"But, Pa," Nilo said, "I can actually see it sinking!"

The remark had come just about when it seemed the ladies had said all they had to say. Mary and Rose sighed. They agreed with Nilo. Watching breathlessly, they clutched each other's arm.

"Pa, isn't it sinking . . . inch by inch?" Nilo spoke again, solemnly, almost begging to be believed.

"Why, that's right! Of course, it's sinking!" the three Adevas exclaimed.

"And nobody's doing anything about it!" Nilo seemed terror-stricken. "What could have happened, Pa?"

Mr. Lopez could say nothing. He could not explain this if he tried. He realized what Nilo wanted; he felt the urgency in the boy's words, in his asking to be believed and the derelict explained away. But Mr. Lopez had no explanation to make here any more than for all he had done to conceal his having failed the boy. He knew that he could not lie to him or about him any longer. The time had come when he could protect him no more with excuses and fabrications. How much further could he go? He would run short of college deans and cigars and Panama Canals, and those little half-truths you said about them that made each day pass sufferably. You could fashion make-believe to order; but, oh, not life, complete with its mystery and loneliness. And he had other sons to see through as well, not to mention the young girl now in grade school—and a fifth offspring yet to come. Of one thing he was certain; with all five of them to look after, you could grow hardened enough. And once you've acquired the callousness, Mr. Lopez thought, how dreadful it all becomes. Thank God, he could see that.

The ferry was clearing the channel and leaving the island now. He could see that too. The green underbrush, the white beach, the derelict itself—was that the mast, a bamboo pole stuck in the water?—all slipped away, and Calapan pier came into view, the zinc roofs of the buildings on the shore garishly white in the sunshine, against the palms on the shoulder of the hill. For a moment Mr. Lopez watched his son Nilo, who stood with his two new friends, their hands on the railing, their eyes shining. A sudden beauty to his being father to this boy possessed him, and he felt that his own eyes were shining too. The deck began to sway—the waves were getting just a bit frisky again—and he sat, steady on that wooden bench and aware of something hard gathering at the core of his being.

"No, not yet," he prayed silently, frightened perhaps by the same terror that had seized Nilo earlier.

But he felt it was already there.

1959

The Wireless Tower

My name is Roberto Cruz.
Honesty is the best policy.
I ought to have a better pair of shoes.
My favorite subject is History, but I like Literature also.
What is a compound sentence?

Wondering what else to say, Roberto Cruz, the troop scribe, counted the number of lines he had used: he had four more to write on before reaching the bottom of the page. He filled these with the names of his father and mother, and those of his brother and sister, and wrote down also their respective dates of birth. Of the four dates, he had difficulty in remembering that of his father. Bert leaned on the wall boards and tried to refresh his memory. He stretched his legs and waited. A soothing comfort ran down his body, from the nape of his neck to his toes.

He watched the wind bending the grass on the side of the mountain directly before him. He felt he could taste in the wind a touch of bay leaf and somehow of cardamom, too. He was reminded of Mother standing before the woodstove emptying a pot of *adobo* into the candy can which, later, the troop, from Scoutmaster Ponte down, devoured to the last tidbit.

Then, forming a lump in his throat—the day and the month of his father's birth. He was not quite sure about the year. But I'm now fifteen, he reasoned; Father married when he was twenty-five. Bert added the two numbers and finally worked out a solution.

The wall stood at his back, an old wall. The cottage, which was to have served as the home of the caretaker of the radio station, had never been occupied. At Bert's feet the boards were covered with the sandlike woodworm droppings from the ceiling. Bert pulled up his knapsack, which had lain at his feet; now he had a pillow. He pushed himself up, and the wall creaked again.

The porch banisters resembled railings for a strip of fence in an abandoned pasture. Nothing obscured Bert's view of the mountainside. It was a pleasant April afternoon, steeped in sunshine. There had been a plan, Bert had heard, to set up a radio station here. Somehow it had not come off. Bert wondered if a rich deposit of rust, like the woodworm in the lumber, had been heaped at the foot of the tower. The structure seemed to hold up, though. Already there was a legend about it: lightning had split the rod at the top. It must have been quite a storm. Bert decided he would go and find out.

He laid his notebook flat on the floor and made a rough sketch of the tower. He rigged up the drawing with the crisscrossing steel strands; the real tower, his model, rose a good hundred and twenty steps heavenward. As he counted, his eagerness mounted. He did not complete the sketch. Hurriedly, he jabbed a vertical line at the top of his steel structure. He marked it with an "X." At the bottom of the page he wrote out a reminder:

To Whom it May Concern:
I'll be up there.

He signed his name simply, *Bert Cruz*. He gave his address:

27 Real Street
Buenavista, Buenavista

Then, smiling to himself, he got up and looked around for a small rock. He found one at the foot of the three-runged steps of the cottage porch. He played with the rock a while, tossing it in the air and catching it, now with his right hand and then with his left.

He walked back to where he had left his knapsack, counting the times he held the rock in the cup of his left palm. At least five times!

His notebook lay beside the knapsack. He picked it up and ran through the pages without looking at them.

Butterflies, birds, fishes, trees and flowers lived like immortal beings in those pages. Bert had an image in the back of his mind of the neat little sentences that he had filled the other pages with. He tried to remember when it was that he had gotten into the habit of putting down things that way, but he couldn't.

He placed the notebook on top of his knapsack and the small rock on top of the notebook, opened on the page where he had written his message. Then, whistling, he walked down to the yard, over the rickety floorboards of the porch, past the ruins of the steps.

The nearest shaft of the tower was the one to the south and was twenty-five steps away. The four of them rose from a base of perhaps seven hundred square feet. Robust concrete blocks anchored each shaft to the mountain. The story was that there ought to have been two towers. People said the second tower was to have risen about five hundred feet, farther to the north. There the hilltop leveled off less flatly than here on the south. Bert wondered not so much why this other tower did not get built at all but rather how the mountain would look with the two towers. He imagined the two towers making conversation with the stars. He thought of the words they might have said to each other, like two friends sitting in the dark, rocking their chairs gently, thinking they had all of forever to themselves.

Now the other steel seemed almost real. Bert closed his eyes for a moment, afraid to see it in the sunshine standing against the blue of the afternoon sky. Pressing his eyelids, he tried to throw off the vision. He did not want it at all. It wouldn't do to ever get mixed up. He realized that in his notebook he had sketched only one tower.

The line of steps hung on the east side. The first rung was about nine feet from the ground. He had to jump a little to reach the bar. He let go, remembering that he had to roll up his sleeves. He folded the cuffs carefully and got his arms clear up to his biceps. Then he reached for the first bar again. He felt it smooth in his hand. He chinned his way upward, pulling in his hips to get some momentum.

By swinging his legs forward and locking in his feet fast behind the big shaft, he was able to let go of one hand and make a good try for the second bar.

The steps were a foot apart. The vertical bars that had held the rungs were a foot wide and ran parallel. Unlocking his feet, Bert caught the swing of his body by slipping his whole arm through and, quickly keeping himself upright on the ladder, a wee strip of skin between his legs got pinched rather tight. He wished he had rolled up his trousers, too; but now that the skin kept hurting he was glad he had not done it.

He realized that he still had his shoes on. It was a canvas pair, all black except for the soles, which were red. He raised his left foot and unknotted and loosened up the lace. He bent over, still safely arm-locked, and pushed the shoe off, tugging from the heel. In like manner, he shed off the other shoe.

This, on hitting the grass, tumbled off miraculously toward its mate. Bert thought this was an omen. He felt that if he had so wished, both shoes might have come together side by side, as in a window display.

But the thought of omens disturbed him. He looked away and saw the portion of the roof where several of the galvanized iron sheets had been wrenched loose by the wind. His eyes followed the gutter that cut an angle with the porch roof. Then his gaze dropped, and he saw his knapsack and the notebook, pale white, stuck under the weight of the rock.

Without being aware of it, Bert had gained ten more steps. He cleared an additional twenty without looking at the cottage again. Resting, he locked his arms onto the step that came level with his shoulder.

He did not realize how far up he had reached until he saw, beyond the trees on the south side of the mountain, the road that led to the town. He followed the road as if he were going home. Suddenly he lost his way in the trees. When he found the road again, it was behind a dark grove of mangoes. The rustle of the leaves seemed to reach him, and somehow this frightened him. It was of course the form that the sound of the wind took, perhaps as it went past the shafts as if these were broken bits of wire. At this thought, Bert got frightened. He climbed yet higher, though. Something seemed at stake. Feeling numbed in the arches of his bare feet, he slipped his leg over one step to rest, as if he were mounted on a horse.

The road passed some bamboos and looked like a strip of tree bark that bunched them up. Then it turned to the beach and went past the town cemetery. The gray walls appeared like the line of barren paddy in a field. Because the tombstones were uniform, the field did not resemble a strip of riceland. But it well could have, judging from the length and turns of the paddy. The wind was brisk now, and it seemed to bend the things that cropped up on the ground and which Bert identified as crosses.

He left his saddle now and diverted his attention to the town slaughterhouse, which was set on a rock that jutted out onto the blue harbor. There was an interisland ship at anchor, the *Nuestra Señora del Rosario*. The superstructure was unmistakable, hooded though it was with what looked like black canvas. Even the bridge had a forbidding shape. The hill was black, too, and the men who crowded the pier looked as if they had only heads and no bodies whatever.

The road through the pier area rose black with mottled gray blots, where moving objects, which Bert identified as carts drawn by carabaos, ranged in a shadow. The wide canopy of zinc, which was the Stevenson copra warehouse, might have glittered away like a great slab of silver. Actually, a cloud hung low over it, enshrouding the building with sheets of the dullest lead.

Bert looked up once. Huge masses of clouds, odd forms heavy like rocks, and as rugged at the edges, hung in a shelf over him. The wind chilled his back. It did not sing past the shafts but began, it seemed, to tap the rivets loose. His feet confirmed their steadiness, though. Now the black ship at anchor in the harbor seemed to get smaller and smaller. The crowd at the wharf had begun to disperse, and the dark spots scattered into the town until at last the streets seemed bare.

The wind turned. It came straight at his face, now washing it clean. It seemed intent on removing some dirt behind his ears. Then it began to scrub his hair and scalp. It rubbed his eyes and cheeks and neck. He felt the sensation of bathing in dry water.

The more steps he cleared the more intense the sensation became. He felt shriven, the dry water of wind having neatly cleansed him. He once saw a movie in which there was a doctor scrubbing his hands and arms interminably. He felt exactly as if he were being cleaned up in that way.

Then it came, a searing ache in the balls of his feet. It rose and seized his knees, gripping them as if with clamps. The wind grew still suddenly. Sweat beaded on his back and across his waist, like a cross. His brow was dry, nothing dimmed before his eyes; but he felt that tears would come any moment. He waited, making three steady steps, locking in his arm each time.

He felt he was no equal to the landscape around him, to the rising and sinking of the ground below. For the first time he thought that perhaps it would be better not to climb any higher. To steady himself he looked up at the clouds that lay in a shelf above him. An imaginary plumb line was being lowered for him, to provide him a bearing. But, suddenly, the line seemed fastened to the tip of the tower and, indeed, became the vertical rod that he must reach. He canted his head, wondering why the rod seemed to move. This was caused, he suspected, by his faulty way of looking.

He could not look long enough, though, to ascertain exactly what the trouble was. His sweat was heavier now, the pain in his bones had spread to his muscles. His calves knotted in tight bow lines and figure-eights. Even his neck seemed held in some awful knot; or, rather, in that series of knots. He laid his chin upon a near step, thinking that in this way he could rest. But his teeth began to chatter.

He held his jaw steady, and then, feeling that his strength had returned, he pressed on, gaining three more steps, then five more, locking in thrice in each case. This gave each foot a much longer spell of rest than before. He discovered he could throw the entire weight of his body alternately on each foot. He felt the pull of the earth coming hard, but the lock counteracted that, and suddenly he felt light.

There was nothing now between him and the rod but a narrow ledge. Somehow he had no desire to reach beyond. It was as if he had brought along this desire like loose change in his pocket. He searched for it now, but nothing jingled there. He felt again the weight about his sweat-beaded back and waist, and he could have slipped earthward from its drag alone, only he had now his hands on the ledge.

He knew from the tautness of his leg muscles that he had made it. He could feel the base of the steel rod now with the tips of his fingers. He closed his eyes for joy. He reached far out, farther out—for joy.

Thumb and forefinger clutched the base of the rod. He wished they would meet, but the base was perhaps too large to encircle. The wind began to sing again. He could feel something like strands of the song at the tips of his thumb and forefinger. An entirely new sensation rose from the middle of his back and settled at the base of his skull. It was made of the wind's song, which came without a tune—without sound, even. And it seemed it would last forever.

He heaved over to get into position for another saddle-rest. His easy success was little short of a miracle, he felt. His hand still gripped the base of the rod; and being able to reach farther now, finger- and thumb-tip met at the rugged edges which rose so many inches up the skin of the shaft. The rugged edges followed whichever way he turned. He could feel the grit in his teeth and the tang of split metal on his lips. His nostrils flared. He caught the smell of the rock, sun-bleached, born and bred of the sun's heat on steel. It seemed that the rod breathed.

And it was split. This was incontrovertible; he could speak of it without a doubt. His hands could be preaching it; it was gospel talk. He was dazed by the thought.

Something had been drained off his hands so that now it left no sensation. But in its place was the anticipation of the feel of the crack and the crevice, and of the length of the split. His heart throbbed as if it would never stop.

Bert felt he could not stand it. This was too much to keep for so long. Slowly, and step by careful step, he retraced his ascent. The rock structure of clouds overhead had lifted and soft felt carpets of them seemed to have spread under the sun. He kept his gaze on the town. Now it glowed—roofs, streets, and all.

Even the market place, the schoolhouse and the church, none of which he had minded before, emerged as if from the shadows and called out to him. He saw the creek that ran past the market place and swept its bed dry to the lee of the harbor, and the pebbles glittered as if they were precious stones. Although still at anchor, the ship had moved from her original position. Somehow a lid of water quivered between her hull, now an indifferent gray, and the cliff of the wharf. The red band on her funnel and the three triangular flags that waved from the main mast were a delight. The flags seemed to wave to him. The ship offered her white-painted deck to his gaze, her bridge aglow with brass trimmings. Surely, she was on her way to another voyage. Smoke, white and lazy, emitted this message from the stack, and there was a new-looking crowd—well-wishers gathering at the pier. Bert thought they were all umbrellas and hats, and as he cleared more steps he recognized some hands, waving and waving.

The last few steps were easy. It was as if his muscles had not tightened up so rudely before. He leaped to the ground and sat on the grass and put on his shoes. Then he walked to the edge of the cottage, a little self-consciously—somehow afraid of himself.

He did not wish to hold up his head proudly; he had no desire to get puffed up in any way. He remembered the cemetery and the dark road through the trees he had seen earlier; and he did not care to swing his arms about.

He reached the tumbledown porch and, picking his way carefully, sat beside the knapsack he had left behind. His notebook, with the pencil tied to it, lay as before under the small rock he had used as a weight. He put the rock away.

Leaning once again against the old wall, he heard it creak under his weight. There followed a shower of woodworm droppings from the ceiling, some falling on the notebook in his hand.

He laid the page open on his lap and wet his pencil tip again. Without reading what he had written earlier, he set his pencil on a fresh line.

With this next sentence, he would have six altogether on the page. It would be better to use a new line.

He wrote: *It is true*.

1963

The Lives of Great Men

IT WAS MANY YEARS AGO THAT I WAS IN BUENA-
vista (said our Acting Credit Manager's assistant)—one of
those strokes of good fortune, you know—it was the Company that sent me over. You couldn't have thanked the Chief
enough.

The plane ride, the two hours of grueling heat on the bus,
the twelve miles by ferry to the next island—what did these
difficulties matter? I had learned my three R's in Buenavista.
The small barrio called Hinala, now the site of the airport,
was where Grandfather took us at the close of each school
term. Before a gathering of his cronies, he'd make an occa-
sion of it, showing us off as specimens of a generation better
endowed than his own, a breed equipped for progress. We
could be relied upon to deliver speeches or recite clever little
verses in a language that neither they nor we ourselves really
understood. What my cousins' performances were like I can't
now exactly recall, but mine were not unremarkable. My
Longfellow's "The Psalm of Life," for example, invariably
won applause.

But the poet's homily deceived no one. If Grandfather's
friends got the message, they hardly made it known. "Bravo!"
they'd say, as if indeed they belonged to the *principalia,* clap-
ping their hands in the manner appropriate to members of
that class. And then they'd go on with their drinking—
which was *tuba,* there being no libation within their means
except this one provided by the ubiquitous coconut palm.

As might be expected, Grandfather's cronies resumed by
morning the lives that Longfellow had mildly interrupted;

127

by first light they'd set out as usual for their fish-traps or rice fields. Thus they carried on, burdened by no great faith or ideals, their every gesture showing no traces that the lives of great men had ever touched them.

It did not occur to me at that time that Longfellow was an irrelevance; those command performances inspired in me a terror that blocked out everything. Rescue came now and then only from Uncle Nemesio, whose promptings and encouragement did him proud as Hinala's leading citizen, being in fact the incumbent head-teacher at the barrio elementary school. In fifteen years, he would be retired from government service and, as one of Grandfather's heirs, would host many a tuba-drinking party himself.

My flight took hardly an hour, the palm fronds in the north wind waving a welcome as we landed. Uncle Nemesio was in the crowd to meet the plane, although hardly on my account, to be sure, for I had neither written him nor wired. As it turned out, he had a bad memory. Not until I had given him my nickname did the blank look in his eyes change into recognition.

We walked straight to his house half a kilometer from the airport, beyond the school grounds. It seemed that some festivities had been planned; a bamboo arch had been built at the school gate, and strips of colored paper fluttered from the porch eaves. Boys and girls were rigging with palm leaves the unfinished concrete fence; this consisted of slabs about two meters long and a meter high, each bearing the name of the local gentry who had been importuned into making a donation. You had a feeling that here was a cemetery where true civic-mindedness and generosity lay quietly buried.

The frame house where we used to stay during vacation time now lodged another family—no relation of ours, my uncle emphasized, his lips twitching as he spoke. The property had passed on, in any case, to an aunt of mine, now deceased and survived by a rather improvident son-in-law. Worse, he had no sentiments about the place whatsoever. In short, I should not expect to be put up there for the night.

The property directly across the street from the old place, however, was the portion that fell to Uncle Nemesio as his inheritance. In this way he came by about a hundred and fifty square meters of property, with a nipa house set off from the street by sweetsop trees.

The house was in reality a shack and was oddly appropriate to all concerned. My uncle, now seventy, had become shorter by three inches, it seemed to me. He had, in my aunt, who emerged from the kitchen shed holding a cooking pot in her hand, a gnomelike companion. Her faded orange dress and her long, hemp-yellow hair heightened this impression. Her eyes were deep-set and restless, like those that belonged, or so you imagined, to some figure in storyland.

"Fidelino is now with us. He used to work in Hawaii," Uncle Nemesio said.

The reference was to their son, my bachelor cousin of forty or so; he was in that airport crowd, only I hadn't recognized him.

"The two of them, father and son . . . that's all they do," my aunt said. "You would think that the governor, or somebody with a basketful of food or a trunkful of money, was coming to help us out."

The remark sounded like a familiar grudge, its point much too blunted from endless dibbling. In any case, my Uncle Nemesio had by now taken off his shirt and had climbed to a bench by the window.

Fastened to the post and one of the rafters, and thus held somewhat above eye level, was a small transistor radio. He devoted his attention to this object presently, turning this knob and that with great care. He became so overwhelmingly enraptured by the music, it was as though I might just as well not have arrived.

Except for the bench and the low center table, the room was bare. Held down upon the table top by two square feet of glass was a spread of snapshots, my cousin Fidelino's and, quite likely, those of his Hawaiian friends.

The shack itself seemed about ready to fall apart; but, quite literally, the lives of great men held it together, in defiance to all conceivable forces that bring things to naught. For here, in makeshift frames hung against the slant of the roof and the wall, was a gallery of our illustrious ones. Strands of hemp fiber, from pieces of string that held the frames in place, quivered in the wind. These pictures, doubtless, had once graced some page or magazine cover. Here now, at one end of the row, was a pensive Abraham Lincoln, and at the other, an amused John F. Kennedy. In a frame also all his own, a proud Manuel L. Quezon stood in white riding breeches and leather boots, in the middle of a rice paddy. A beam of mangrove wood set apart three other frames. The first was that of Elpidio Quirino, who bestowed on me an enigmatic smile. Alongside was Manuel L. Roxas in his solemn best. Yet another was a group picture of the very heroes of the nation: Jose Rizal, Marcelo H. del Pilar, and Mariano Ponce—all in heavy overcoats, so cold it must have been in Madrid during that winter of their exile.

My cousin Fidelino had arrived. "When we saw you," he said, "all I could think of was whether there would be fish in the fish corral." He took off the rather sporty knit shirt he had worn to the airport. "Let me go to the water this very minute." And with that he dropped out of sight.

I had always remembered him as a little boy who ran around as likely as not without trousers and who did not have enough stretches of beach to cover in full trot. Now he had on those dark blue dacron trousers, the cuffs folded six inches high and weighted down with sand.

My aunt joined us at this juncture. "Clothes are all that he brought home from Hawaii. So what do his uncles and cousins do? Here they come and they walk off with a shirt or two every time. It won't be long before he'll be as naked as before. The fish corral used to give us plenty of fish," she added, "but we are now in the wrong time of year. In two months, things could be better, though."

Fidelino had left without a word. I thought he might have asked me to join him, at least, and that he did not rather disturbed me. He might have wanted me to see how things were down at the beach.

I felt I had to go myself. The *amihan* had stopped; the palm fronds hardly moved. A little to the right, on the horizon, lay Kalatong Point, reminding me of countless golden-red snappers that had often got the better of my patience. The slow oncoming twilight here could play tricks on the imagination. When the tide was down, the waterline showed markedly on the palings, creating the illusion of another horizon.

But I knew these waters; I knew Kalatong. The fairest of women lived there, according to legend. Kalatong trees were all of the same height, and beautiful music awaited you in the forest. On the eve of the feast of Santa Catalina, a white ship dropped anchor off the point. Exactly at the stroke of twelve, on the eve of Good Friday, you must smear your eyelids with beeswax and then hurry to the beach, for you might just see then the captain's launch heading straight for the shore. It'd be he who could take you to some country far away, where you'd make your fortune. Did Fidelino know all this?

He presently appeared and began wading toward the shore. For the most part the water was waist-deep, and it was not long before he proudly held up against the twilight sky, to show me, a string of wrasses and snappers.

"In two months, we'll have sardines and garfish here . . . a whole lot of them!"

We had supper soon afterwards and, too tired to do anything or go anywhere, I decided to turn in early. I did remember the bed with Fidelino's suitcases stacked beneath. A girl of ten, or thereabouts, now lay curled up on it—she must have been there all this time, only I had not noticed. The thatched wall and her sleeping mat seemed to have merged; in the darkness neither could be set apart from the other. I had been deaf to her intermittent coughing; now her efforts to clear her throat were developing into spasms. In any case, she was a presence, an identity to be accounted for.

"A bad cold . . . that's all," my aunt explained. "It's been a week now. She should be up and about, but she stayed too long in the sun yesterday."

The girl, meanwhile, had begun rolling up her mat. In a minute she had moved to the other room, the bundle too heavy-looking for her.

"Time for bed," my aunt now turned to Uncle Nemesio. He had been comfortable there on his bench for so long, sitting with one knee upraised, and did not seem ready to be dislodged. But slowly he rose, as obedient as a little boy.

"Auntie," I protested, for what she was up to dawned on me. "Let me sleep anywhere."

But she would not hear of it. The girl could go elsewhere—the matter was settled! The spot under the bench would be just right for her.

But how was I to sleep? I felt terrible over her yielding the bed. Perhaps she had done it of her own accord; perhaps not. The thatch shingles gave out a musty odor. Hordes of lice seemed to have taken possession of the sleeping mat, and I knew they had all of me to crawl over. I heard someone in the yard—Fidelino. And my aunt was chiding him gently, "Better not make any noise. You'll wake him up."

He was quickly gone, and it was perhaps then that I finally dropped off to sleep, though I must have wakened later, for I thought I saw him change and leave again, now in a bright red shirt, off into the night. I might have imagined the color—I don't know. And then sometime afterward I heard some faint and melancholy music. Could this be a string band or a phonograph? Uncle Nemesio's transistor radio, perhaps?

Ah, the music from Kalatong forest, I said to myself, fully awake by now.

My aunt was in the room to fetch something. "There's a school benefit dance out there," she said, when she heard me stir. "Someone came a while ago asking about you."

I couldn't imagine having anything to do with a school benefit dance. "What did he want?" I asked.

"To know if you could join them. I said you were sound asleep. You were, weren't you? Oh, how you snored!" She gave a little laugh. "A donation for the school . . . that's what they're after. You don't go for that, I know. As to your cousin, he's one who'll not allow himself to be left out. He pledged money for an entire section of the school fence."

After this remark, she said nothing more. In the meantime, the distant music became one with the waves of throbbing sound that the crickets raised in the sweetsop trees.

The bus to the ferry landing forty kilometers away arrived about seven the next morning. It pulled up in front of a food stall across the yard from the local airline office and waited there for northbound passengers. There was only time for coffee and a piece of rice cake, which both my uncle and Fidelino declined when asked to join.

In Buenavista, I dispatched as quickly as I could the business I had been sent to look into and was back at the Hinala airport in good time for my flight back to Manila. My aunt had joined Uncle Nemesio at the airport to see me off; Fidelino turned up, too.

"People asked why you were not at the dance," he said.

"What excuse did you give?"

"You were too tired, I said."

And that touched me somewhat, and I thought I could pay him back in kind with some thoughtful gesture of my own. As a matter of fact, it must have been in the back of my mind for some time. "There's a good chance you might make good money here . . . if you like," I began.

"How?" he asked, rather puzzled.

"You might start a poultry farm. You could ship fresh eggs to the city every day."

But he laughed off the idea. "Oh, we're quite all right as it is. We really are. In two months, the fish corral will be bringing in money."

"If not a poultry farm, then a piggery. Something . . . anything!"

"Last night there was a big tide," Fidelino said. "We had a catch of five kilos of wrasses. Off it went by the first bus this morning to Buenavista. . . . Later, there will always be income from the coconuts."

Yes, Grandfather's coconuts, I could have said aloud. But something made me keep it all to myself. I could also have said: After Hawaii, didn't you learn a thing or two? Have you no ambition at all? Don't you want to be better off than you are now?—But I recalled the evening before, the music from the schoolhouse; and, as if rejecting the legend of the tall trees and the white ship off Kalatong Point, I heard myself giving expression to something else. It might have been the most gross of all my thoughts.

"What's wrong with the girl?" I asked guardedly.

"Measles."

It was my aunt who spoke; she had overheard me. "If it's catching it that you fear," she said, "don't worry. You had it years ago. Don't you remember? You can't catch it now."

But, of course, I had forgotten. And once again she smiled in that gnomish way of hers. Did she know what I had been thinking? I had been mistaken, suspecting that she and Fidelino had been at odds. They had in fact been allies in good standing. Who, for instance, was the girl but a love child? Fidelino's, most naturally! How unfortunate for the girl, had Fidelino's mother—my aunt, that is—not been there to look after her while he was away in Hawaii. And who would the girl's mother be? And, if I knew, what then? Would that be knowledge that should matter?

The many questions in my mind could only mean one thing: they emphasized the distance that had come between us. All I could do now was to trust that I be forgiven for my coarse efforts at making contact.

But my remorse was shortlived. The plane had already arrived. In the ensuing commotion, I couldn't think of anything worth saying. Even small talk eluded me. All three of them—Fidelino, my uncle, and my aunt—stood at the edge of the crowd that awaited the moment of departure; and from the ramp I waved to them, much in the manner of those great ones whose photographs had appeared in newspapers and magazines . . .

That pose (continued our Acting Credit Manager's assistant) I might have managed well enough then—and now might never quite live down.

1964

The Popcorn Man

IT WAS ONE AND A HALF HOURS OF DUST AND BUMPY stretches ("Sorry, people," their driver would say), and then you had the sun to your left until the turn of the road near San Miguel. This was the chief commercial center in those parts; it was also where a freeway of sorts began, a demonstration piece built under the auspices of an ICA program and which led straight to the U.S. Army camp in the shelter of the Sierra Madre.

By three o'clock you were billeted at one of the quonsets clustered near the Camp Sierra Madre Officers Club, the CSMOC of the marquee. Today a huge sign announced that a two-weeks field-commanders' conference on guerrilla techniques was in progress. In the acacia grove beyond the quonsets, you heard the orioles calling against the throbbing cicada music; you had always thought you could depend on them to turn up if you didn't mind missing once in a while the lilt in their voices.

Thus began the routine of the professoriate of the Sierra Madre Air Force Base University Extension Program. A quick visit to the rest room, and the men in the group joined their women colleagues at the quonset across the yard. The ladies for their part, having discarded their travel-rumpled cotton frocks and changed into fresh ones, would lead the group to the Officers Club for *merienda*. There, apple pies were often favored. Oh, but it could well be doughnuts today, although you were not supposed to rub that in; they had served vulgar purposes enough. Anything for a good laugh had become the rule with them, and their attempts at humor had been excessive.

During the previous semester, Miss Elena's favorite had been strawberry ice cream, and Mrs. Dinglasan's, pecan pie. Young Assistant Professor Perez had been partial to chicken sandwiches; Professor Leynes, to grilled cheese and fresh potato chips, lettuce and tomato. And then came a discovery: he could manage on popcorn. At his disposal, free of charge, was an entire basketful usually. He had only to reach across the table and he could have his fill the next moment of those crunchy, butter-flavored pops. Yes, why not? The CSMOC provided its members with a generous supply, and Professor Leynes was a card-bearing member, as were all the professoriate in the Extension Program. The regulations required it, and you had to get the regulations to work on your side. Professor Leynes's discovery was crucial, indeed. He had now only to raise his arm, bend a little forward, and without so much as a "Pardon my boardinghouse reach" prove that many things in this world come free and in abundance.

The merienda was a function that all of them enjoyed, if somewhat grudgingly. While too heavy as tea, it was too light as supper. But at best it offered a mirror of their characters. Here, instead of saying "Please pass the cream," Mrs. Dinglasan, preferring her own brand of flippancy, could say: "Hello, milk!" Leynes had given up hope that she would ever learn. Young Perez, whose subject was Philippine History, had caught on early enough in the game. He had learned to say "Hello, sugar!" During the previous term, Miss Elena, who then taught Economics, had two classes in a row and had particularly no time for a full-fledged meal; she had to resort to fried chicken "to go." This order, though, was discontinued. She had since been obliged to move supper to merienda-time, asking for steak eagerly, only to discover that it worked like a drug. At her first class, she'd turn up sluggish and dull; and at her second, embarrassingly sleepy. She had to forgo the early steak dinner altogether. If only she'd try popcorn, Professor Leynes suggested. But Miss Elena would not hear of it. She would have none of Leynes's style.

"No offense meant, mind you!"

"That's quite all right," Leynes laughed it off.

But, in truth, he felt rather sluggish himself this otherwise fine afternoon. While drinking coffee, which came free as well, he tried to be cheerful. "Hello, cream!" he said. But something had gone wrong; he couldn't put his finger on it. The best he could do was to empty the popcorn container with determination and vigor.

After the merienda, some twenty minutes later, he retired with his colleagues to the bookshop. Today, as always, they might have been hungry children standing before a display of pastries. For the books could only be purchased with MPCs, a currency exclusively for bona fide officers. Browsing was allowed, however; and Leynes was satisfied with that.

Still the injustice rankled; and it stayed with him as he left his companions for the comfort room. There a haggard, fiftyish face stared at him from the mirror above the washstand. Taking note of the bags under the stranger's eyes, he moistened his thumb and forefinger with the warm tap water and worked the eyebrows and temples until the soothing feeling went deep down, it seemed to him, to the very hollow of this stranger's cheeks.

On the way out, he paused at the weighing machine. A hundred and thirty-two pounds, it said. The job, it might be said, did not particularly agree with him. On the contrary, it exacted a heavy toll on his energies. Here was the result of two years of service. He walked away from the comfort room and proceeded to the main hall of the Club, conscious that he had lost those sprightly steps that the heavy carpet had known before. Only one advantage might be pointed out, he thought: he had been able to keep his weight down.

Freshman Composition, Section A, occupied a corner room at the east end of the last quonset on the row. The entire cluster of quonsets was called Benton Education Center, in memory of a general who had died in a plane crash some years back. It was, by day, Benton School for Camp Sierra Dependents. Accordingly, the room Leynes occupied had been outfitted for fifth-grade history. A rack off in one corner housed a collection of maps called "Rand-McNally's U.S. History in Color." The seats were curved for teenage buttocks; a pink-enameled refrigerator stood at the far end of the room, while a huge electric fan favored one corner with a low drone. It was impossible to look around and not imagine a spinsterly blonde demanding to know, smiling: "What and where was the Louisiana Purchase?"

Amidst the customarily indifferent greetings, Leynes entered his room. He acknowledged them perfunctorily and then began the session by passing around for signatures the blue attendance sheet required by Benton Education Center authorities. Muller, Schneider, Brown, Phelps—he ran through the names on the sheet. These were the stalwarts. Hammond and Metallous—in two out of six meetings you could count on the pair being absent. But they had turned up today: they were as big as life. He remembered Weeks, who had died in a road accident; and Wilson, who had gone on TDY and, unable to catch up with the work, had elected to drop out. There had been others who, before you could become familiar with their faces, simply disappeared without a trace. And there was Harris, handsome and clever Jane Harris, a girl from Georgia, who had been both a joy and a pain. She had been quick to see virtue in grammar but continued to split her infinitives and refused to see a run-on sentence even if one were shoved right in her face. And she hedged, equivocated, argued—the times she had flabbergasted him—using every weapon in her arsenal so that her innocence would not be violated. Worse, she chewed gum and popped it every so often like a seven-year-old.

Leynes braced up and said: "We have the subjunctive mood for today, don't we? On page 374 of the textbook is a very interesting chart. You probably had a chance to look at it . . . Well, we shall see . . . Miss Harris, can you explain how the verb *to be* is used in the subjunctive?"

The university car collected the professoriate for the short trip to the Officers Club for dinner, and the company now included Miss Elena. She had a better schedule this semester.

For the delectation of the company, Leynes was about to remark, thinking of young Perez: "Which reminds me . . . your students have been making a tally of the number of times you say 'Now' in the course of the lecture hour, and I overheard one of them saying you scored seventy-five tonight. No, eighty-three, said another . . ." But Leynes decided to keep the matter to himself. For Jane Harris occupied his mind. He had had trouble getting her to accept that it was permissible to use the indicative form of the verb in a sentence in the subjunctive mood. She had got back at him, throwing up her arms, exclaiming: "Oh, well, you know the language better than we do!" He had had to explain the point patiently. He was merely making the textbook clear, he had said. And at this juncture she favored him a sullen look. Then, as if by accident, her book fell to the floor, causing a quite unusually shattering noise. She bent over to pick it up, making no effort to prevent a remarkable display of bosom—verily to assuage his annoyance, Leynes said to himself. Guerrilla tactics!

But, of course, he could not be disposed of that readily. "Last week," Leynes said, addressing no one in particular, "they couldn't figure out whether to say 'one of the many who have died,' or 'one of the many who has died' . . ."

"Neither could I, frankly," said Miss Elena.

"Can," said Perez. "Correction, please!"

Miss Elena overlooked that. "And I'm hungry. I bet it's crowded at the Club just now. I hate to be one of the many who will have to wait . . ."

"There . . . you got it!" Leynes said.

"Did I?" she said, pertly.

It being Monday, they ordered the special dinner, which, before seven, cost only seventy cents. On other evenings, it was a dollar and twenty-five—quite a drain, Leynes recognized.

And it was so early they didn't have to wait long to be served. Judging by standards with which the group had become familiar and had learned to accept, tonight's waiters were prompt and polite. You caught no hint of condescension toward their own countrymen.

When nearly all of them were through, they heard Leynes exclaim: "Why, if it isn't the old son of a gun!" And to cries of "Who?" . . . "Who's it?" . . . he replied: "C. B. Carlos himself . . . you don't know C. B. Carlos? He made quite a name, writing those pieces about the Base, about territorial rights, race prejudice . . . that sort of thing. You'd think he'd be a marked man hereabouts. But there, take a look at him . . . quite the contrary!"

The company was impressed. Two ladies and their officer

escorts made up Carlos's group five tables away. In his dark business suit, he was the very image of success.

"We were in school together," Leynes went on, his enthusiasm seemingly boundless. He's a big shot now. That's what he's become."

"If I'm not mistaken, he made the articles into a book," said Miss Elena.

"A timely subject, certainly. How were the reviews?" Mrs. Dinglasan asked, anxious to contribute to the conversation.

"Raves," Leynes replied. "If you people will excuse me, let me go to congratulate him."

Miss Elena and Mrs. Dinglasan waited at the lobby for the party to collect before returning to the Center. As for Perez, he did the intelligent thing: he returned to the car—to listen to the radio.

When Leynes rejoined them, he said: "Anyone for a bit of night life? Carlos is inviting us."

"Why didn't he ask us directly?" Miss Elena wanted to know.

"He has delegated that to me," Leynes said.

"Then we can't! We shouldn't?" Mrs. Dinglasan demurred. "No, not in a place like this. We schoolma'ams might be mistaken for something else."

Her matronly air was not lost on Leynes. "What prudes," he wanted to say. But already the car had pulled up to the Benton Education Center, and they rushed to their classrooms.

Leynes's class was Intro. to Lit.—where Bauer, Montoya, Richards, and some others were the fairly steady scholars. Hibbit was on TDY, Richards reported. Leynes had hoped that Johnson might turn up tonight. It was to Johnson that he had wanted to explain the week before that you didn't stay away from Conrad's *The Nigger of the Narcissus* simply because of *that* word in the title. Literature was Literature. It served its purpose best by following the doctrine of proper words in proper places. It was just too bad that Johnson hadn't been in attendance more often. This was one problem with the entire extension program. Absences were rampant; you couldn't be too conscientious about your work. It was rare that you gave a failing mark. You were only too happy when you met the required class sizes, relieved when each class hour was over, and gratified when the term itself came to an end. Appointment to the extension professoriate had become an expression of patronage, the regular salary increases having become difficult to come by. What a stink the program would probably raise, Leynes thought, once a typewriter like C. B. Carlos's were put to work.

Carlos was, in fact, already outside waiting in his car. The gesture overwhelmed Leynes. "I'll show you around, I will," Carlos was saying. "You really don't know this place, do you?"

Indeed, he did not, Leynes said; and they were out of the Benton Education Center compound shortly.

Someone in a scooter came abreast of them part of the way. Bauer—Leynes recognized the driver. Bauer had remarked that T. S. Eliot's *Murder in the Cathedral* demonstrated "a case of suicide." That was the young man's phrase for it, an easy conclusion; nevertheless it had been welcome, since hardly anyone had read the assignment well enough to formulate any ideas about it. And now, suddenly, Bauer, his white helmet gleaming in the dark, slipped away before their very eyes, a young man across whose sky a vision had flashed. In a breath, he was transformed into a nothingness amidst the agitated whir of cicadas in the acacias that lined the road.

Some such disintegration could befall him, Leynes thought with a start. Unless he could get a grip on things, it would be his lot. He now knew why he had become excited over this chance encounter with Carlos. There was a subversive quality to their friendship.

"I'd like to do some writing, too," he said.

It came just like that; Leynes was mildly surprised over how he had managed it. And perhaps the announcement might have been helped by the music that the cicadas made, wave upon trembling wave—.

"What will you write about?" Carlos had caught it.

"This place," Leynes said. "I've had this assignment two years now."

A bolt of lightning struck in the east, momentarily setting a portion of the sky ablaze. As if Carlos construed Leynes's statement as a challenge to the authority behind those newspaper articles, a similar protestation quickly followed:

"I've lived in nearby San Miguel all these years myself. The tons and tons of information I have about this place, about all the people hereabouts."

Leynes gave it no importance, for he had not meant to pose a challenge or offer competition in any way. He pursued, instead, a different tack: "One might write about our being here, about what we've to go through here."

It had begun to drizzle. He held up his palm to feel the rain and thought of the task that a person like one with Carlos's gifts might set himself to do—only to realize the next moment that it was actually himself he had in mind.

"Is it as bad as that?" the other said.

"We are educational concessionaires here," Leynes replied. "On the same footing as the barbers and drycleaners." He was moved by the phrase he had stumbled on, "only, instead of goods and services, we vend diplomas."

"Vend, eh?" Carlos chuckled. "I like that."

The visit to Eagle's Roost ("Don't you like the Hawaiian decor?") and the meeting with the culturati, like the club manager and the band leader; the Manhattan in his hand at The Pago-Pago, while couples danced on invisible dimes on the parqueted floor five feet away; the brief look at Lucy's ("You must feel at home here, as I do!"), the swankiest night spot in San Miguel, just outside the gate of the army base—Leynes was struck by the rather harsh quality of life that Carlos offered for his admiration. By the time the rain had stopped, the excursion was over even as the impression it had created deepened.

Uneasy about how to regard him from now on, Leynes sat quietly beside his host in the car that returned him to his billet. Leynes reminded himself that with some sensitive souls, or so he had read somewhere, no experience could be so trivial as to be lost entirely. Like the rain-washed road they were traveling on, he had soaked it all in. Tonight, it might even be asserted, he was being replenished in advance against drought, in the mysterious way Nature does such things. He could be grateful for that. He felt a rash of extravagant fraternal feelings for Carlos such as he had not suspected he was capable of. But something rankled within him, a vast stirring of disaffection. He was troubled by the possibility that Carlos had underestimated him and had thought of him as different from Leynes's own sense of himself—something to be set aright, perhaps once and for all.

"This is awkward of me to ask," Leynes began, "but when do you work, C. B.?" There, he had said it at last. "How do you ever get the chance to sit down at your typewriter?" He could not have sounded more earnest, more anxious—more like himself.

"You don't mean all that, do you?" Carlos sounded puzzled. "Imagine me having to be the one to tell you." He put his arm on Leynes's shoulder. "Anyhow, it'd be a long story if I could tell it at all."

They arrived at the billet shortly, the car wheels grinding to a soggy stop in the overflow from the rain gutter.

"But I really mean it, C. B. Do you do your best work in the mornings? As most others do . . . or so we are told?"

"Come now . . . you must be joking."

Leynes was determined to get an answer. "Do you do your best well into the night, like this . . . in silence like this?"

For, indeed, the quiet was overwhelming. The cicadas were gone; the two of them seemed to be the only souls abroad. They might well have come to some outpost, to the very frontier of a world. It was as though he, Leynes, was to do sentry work here—a lookout pressed into service by a most ennobling sense of mission.

"Now, look," said Carlos, his hands still on the wheel, ". . . as one craftsman to another . . ."

"Yes . . ." said Leynes with bated breath.

Suddenly, the other laughed. "You don't mean to steal my secret, do you?" he said.

When they reached the billet, Carlos stayed nearly a quarter of an hour more with him on the porch, talking shop before driving back to San Miguel. For this Leynes felt grateful. He had come away with the feeling that he, too, would be a success. At Lucy's, someone had asked Carlos, "Isn't your friend the English teacher hungry at all?" and so they had fed him; and now, although too tired to change into pajamas, he just had to for the food had made him feel heavy. It took some effort to move quietly about in the room which he shared with Perez. The sound of dripping water, like a child's sobbing, alerted him to a possibly malfunctioning flushing mechanism in the bathroom. He mounted the bowl cover and fumbled overhead for the offending valve. It was no use. Unaware of the problem, Perez snored soundly enough, an earnest young man underway like a sleek schooner, off across the gulf of dreams.

For how long had it been with Perez that way while he, Leynes wondered, sat restlessly a while, looking around him anxiously as though the room would yield yet more facts and illusions of their lives, some formulas for self-assurance and success—the kind, anyhow, that Carlos achieved? Sorting out his impressions of the evening as though they had been written down on three-by-five note cards, he shuffled and stacked them this way and that, and one particular entry kept turning up:

Leynes, Fermin J. "Fundamentals of Freshman Composition," *Education in Review*, IX:3, pp. 225–236.

His one contribution to scholarship, that; and in a journal that often appeared six quarters late—surely, the journal of either the dead or the dying.

Envy—he must accept it now—envy for C. B. Carlos, newspaperman and author of *Ordeal at Sierra Madre*, welled deep in his soul. Yes, they had been schoolmates; so Carlos had no reason to thrive while he, Leynes, bleached the grammar of U.S. servicemen into presentable whiteness. Perez, Elena, and Dinglasan—they, too, made the laundry concession go. Another gang would be brought in tomorrow— a math instructor, a geology professor, a P.E. man—the Tuesday-Thursday shift. They had been committed, all of them, to being domestics in the academic world; and this was something they had not counted on. It was something extra and, perhaps, considering the circumstances, something to be thankful for. But was there nothing else to aspire to? Surely, there were limitations for Carlos, as well. Leynes had no doubt about that, and he felt anxious for him almost as keenly as for himself. Carlos could be asking his own questions in turn, seeking his own answers.

The flush toilet dripped on, in odd affirmation of Leynes's thoughts, he felt; and sleep seemed reserved only for the young and innocent, untouched by the fairy's wand. Leynes saw himself already transformed, although happily, into the person he had always longed to be: a storyteller, a maker of fables with which to explain away the confusions of his time and place, and whose voice the world could listen to. His disguise as a Freshman Comp. and Lit. instructor he would keep, though not that part of it that turned him into a plodding white-collar. He had made every rule of grammar pay, every nonrestrictive clause, every colon and comma. He had tried to get at Carlos's secret, had he not? So, then, however you looked at it, he snitched. It had come down to that. And not in terms of popcorn alone, you might say. Did not the others snitch also? Did not Miss Elena and Mrs. Dinglasan scrape the saucer clean of butter cubes, and did they not make sandwiches out of those buns and crackers in the bread baskets? Four cubes to every saucer—"For our midnight snack," they said. Still and all, they snitched, as did Leynes himself, and at just that level. There had been that morning when he rolled up half a dozen bathroom paper mats and pocketed two tiny cakes of soap. Because you couldn't be sure you'd be assigned a billet with all the amenities, he had told himself. And how he dreaded athlete's foot!

He heard the car pulling up front, the driver pressing

gently on the horn but just loud enough to make him get up with a start. Already Perez was packing his bag.

"I was thinking, sir," said the young man, "that you could use a few more minutes of sleep. But, oh well, you're up. Did you have a great time?"

Undecided as to whether to boast or simply to seem vague about the experience, Leynes replied: "We just about went everywhere."

He switched on the light himself, glad over Perez's thoughtfulness in any case. From the voices outside, it was clear that Miss Elena and Mrs. Dinglasan were already in the car.

"Who'd have thought they'd be up and about this early?" Leynes said half-aloud.

"We decided last night," Perez filled him in, "that we might have breakfast down the road somewhere, in some *carenderia* where we could order a real nice, heavy Filipino meal for a change. Fried eggs, rice, sausages, chocolate—and not those buns, waffles, and cornflakes at the Club. Aren't you tired of that stuff?"

The way Perez spoke, it seemed as if some soul-searching was required on Leynes's part. He came up with "I can't really say," and said it as simply as he could.

Directly after he had collected his gear he joined the ladies in the car, fitting himself between the two of them in the rear. In a minute they were out of the area, cruising along the acacia-lined park and heading for the camp gate.

"Going home at this hour is the part of this job I like best," Mrs. Dinglasan said. "Don't you feel that way, too?"

"Oh, but I do!" said Miss Elena. She was munching something but went on talking. "Sorry, people. I'm always hungry at this hour, you know."

Those crackers again, thought Leynes. But he couldn't bring himself to be too critical of her. He had begun to feel the chill and hurried to button up at the collar.

"Cold, huh?" Mrs. Dinglasan said, kindly.

"Not quite," Leynes said, touched by her interest.

They were now passing quickly through San Miguel town and leaving behind those zinc-roofed houses and boarded-up shops which in an hour or so would come alive with trade from the camp. Their headlights caught the clusters of grey nipa houses along the road. An open field emerged, then an island of bamboos against the sky, then a peninsula of rice seedlings and a promontory that became all too soon a grove of mango trees. His country, Leynes knew; and not that one back there—where the Carloses triumphed, but which also diminished them, as the cicadas sang their chorus.

From where he sat beside the driver, Perez chirped brightly: "Hello, Highway!"

1963

Crossing Over

OUR BOAT, A FREIGHTER WITH SUGAR FROM NEGROS and hemp from Albay, was to dock at San Francisco; but a longshoremen's strike, we learned, was in progress there and we had to proceed to Oakland instead.

"Isn't there anyone in this bright winter sunshine, anyone I might know?" I said to myself, seeing a little crowd gathering twenty feet below where I stood on the deck, leaning over the railing. I felt as if I needed a miracle.

Someone tapped my shoulder from behind, and said: "Oh, here you are. This is for you."

It was the purser, with a long, light-blue envelope for me. And at once I knew where this had come from: the foundation that had awarded me a fellowship. To set foot in America and to be looked after like that was beyond my wildest dreams. An omnipotence had brought me over and would keep watch all the way.

The letter could not have been more reassuring. It did, in fact, have a hundred-dollar check to tide me over until my regular stipend arrived. Proceed directly to Stanford Village, in Palo Alto, it said.

On the other side of the bay was the big city that I had only seen in pictures—in the mist, a rise of skyscrapers aglitter in the cloud drift of sunshine. To the far south, shrouded with fog, would be Palo Alto.

These distances and directions had remained fixed in my mind for so long, how could I not know them now by heart? But how does one get to Palo Alto from the Oakland pier? It seemed quite an insurmountable problem. At the same time, it did not faze me. My self-confidence was of course without foundation. Down below, on the dock, things were utterly at a standstill on account of the strike.

I did see a pickup pull up close, and the thought occurred to me that it might not be a bad idea to try to get to San Francisco on it.

Did I, perhaps by telepathy, manage to send that message to its driver? He was a middle-aged fellow; a second look, and it seemed he was in fact smiling at me.

In the meanwhile, a tall, gray-haired woman had come up on our deck and, with a smile even more welcoming than that of the old man, she said she'd be happy to give anyone a lift.

She was fifty or so and wore a flouncy skirt and a loose-sleeved blouse weighted down by shell shards and glass beads. A large comb stuck out at the back of her head, keeping in place an ample knot of hair. Over her shoulders was an alpaca shawl. "A witch . . . that's who this is," I told myself.

"Isn't it San Francisco where you're going?"

Her offer should fool no one, I warned myself.

"If it's a ride you're looking for . . ." she tried once more.

"Friends are coming to fetch me," I said—which was a lie, of course.

"Taxis are also on strike."

It did appear so, although no one on board had told us about this. "My friends are coming anyway . . . with their own transport," I assured the old woman.

Words which, I figured, could impress if spoken confidently, which I did—and just about then two men and a girl turned up.

"Oh, I see," said the old one, stepping aside. "Here they are."

But friends of mine, they most certainly were not.

Let me pause here to say that I had not been the only passenger on that freighter. There had been two others, Filipino students like myself—Visayan girls, in their early twenties—and such poor sailors, those darlings. They had been so seasick that I had been cabin boy, deck hand, and brother to them most days of the voyage.

It took some convincing to have them quit their stuffy cabin for the improvised quarters that the captain let them have, an area on the starboard, adjacent to the bridge, where at least they'd feel less cooped up.

But this camping out invited attention. Hardly could the ship's officers avoid hanging around. My role as chaperon seemed predestined; I would have to be ever on the alert, lest an innocent invitation for a viewing of a breathtaking moonrise over the Pacific could become a not too unromantic scene. Being Filipinas, of their time and place, the two girls could not be exposed to casual friendships, let alone shipboard romances. They seemed to have understood this, and they felt I understood this, too. That they had a compatriot seemed a godsend. Before me was a duty to be nobly discharged.

How I came by this foreknowledge and sense of obligation puzzles me today. At that time, I thought nothing of it. Shipboard adventures were the stuff of Hollywood movies, but my complicity in holding romance and life at bay— where did that come from?

Although a sword may hang too long as a piece of wall decoration, it cannot but fit as snugly as before into the tooled leather scabbard that, in the first place, had been fashioned for it. This I see now. But at that time, all I knew was that I aspired to no reward for my bother. Back of my mind, however, to be quite honest, I believe I had hoped that my being helpful could count toward something, although what this might be I had no idea.

The friends the old woman referred to were people who had come to fetch the two girls. How they had located the boat amazed me. In any case, they were no sooner on board than the two girls were gone, off with their two offerings of what some alleged to be the pristine innocence that I had been asked to preserve. And I felt considerable rancor over their allowing themselves to be whisked away like that. They might have offered to take me along—their friends had cars!—even only as a gesture. Or they might have asked how I planned to get to the city on my own. I would answer in some indeterminate way, but their show of interest would suffice. They could have easily made the effort, taking into consideration the fact that I was at least a countryman, if nothing more.

The hurt was there. At that time, I had no explanation for it, but perhaps now I have. They came from rich Visayan families, from some hacienda in the heartland of Negros, back home. I had been the sharecropper's son allowed to linger about the plantation house. My feelings of betrayal would have been beyond their grasp. If at that time I had already identified it and had somehow let on how it hurt, they would not have been amused.

What with these feelings and then the offer that the old woman made, it seemed I was being set up by the Fates. The old man had been waiting on the dock, in his pickup. As in folktales, it is shrewdness that often comes to one's rescue. In this instance, I had lost neither the peasant's talent for it nor that of the boy, whose place was the back porch steps of the hacienda house, that tin-roofed island in the sea of noble cane waving in the sun.

The old woman had disappeared, and the man in the

pickup materialized before me in her stead. It was all I could do now to dissemble and assume an air. I inquired what it would cost me, baggage and all, to be taken to the city. He named a sum that seemed reasonable enough. I did not try to drive a bargain.

We were on our way in no time. It would be only a forty-minute ride, he assured me.

He was talkative from the start. He pointed out the landmarks as if he were a regular tourist's guide. I did observe almost immediately that we had taken the lower deck of the Oakland Bay Bridge. Why not the upper one? I wondered.

Up till then I did not associate his ebullience with any plan of action, but I couldn't but think back on the events of the last twenty minutes: my rejection of the crone; and this man's waiting, his making a move only after the two girls had gone; and now my being utterly on my own—why, here was quite a stratagem. The old man could only mean harm. And, worse, the situation struck me as familiar. I had seen it all in the movies!

Instead of a clear and open view of the bay, as might have been the case had we taken the upper deck of the bridge, all that I could see from my seat in the pickup, with the man at my left, were girders, steel beams, and huge cables: hardly an introduction to America to be enthusiastic about.

Added to this was the thought that the old man could knock me cold and then toss me into the bay. The light traffic could make that a cinch. He'd have to rob me, I'd imagined. Well, he'd only find a few loose bills and the check. There was very little he could do, really. In his disgust, he'd panic. He had merely wasted time on me and would then have to get rid of me entirely, shoving me overboard at the first opportunity.

While his crime in all its heinousness shaped up in my

mind, my fingers, seemingly working on their own, were busy fumbling for my name-card, attaching one to the inner lining of my jacket. Where I found a safety pin for this operation, on all counts a not uncomplicated one, I couldn't say. But that was one handy safety pin, all right! I took a deep breath to enjoy my success. Surely, my name-card couldn't come away or fall or get torn off, however my body tumbled into the water. I would be fished out before the turn of the tide, as a newspaper account would put it. The old man would read the story in his evening paper; right there before his eyes would be a picture of the body of his Filipino! And not just anyone, either. For this one had taken pains to leave his identity in no doubt. In the morgue, some witty coroner's assistant would have a ready tribute for him: "Ah, the guy knew! Identity, to him, was of the essence!"

This drama unfolded on a stage entirely all its own in my mind—while, on another level of actuality, I made small talk with the old man. I must have dropped words and phrases in the conversation that let on that I had come to America to study. As we drove on, I observed that he couldn't seem to have enough of me. He'd look me over from head to foot, as if he had to be certain that there was nothing more to this hapless hacienda yardboy he was taking into the city.

I did have in my suitcase a light pinstripe woolen suit, a gift from an uncle. The package had reached me in Manila just in time. It was a suit he might have worn for a Sunday stroll at Portsmouth Square or down Broadway. He was somewhere in the Pacific, though, on his merchant ship at that time of day, a mess boy answering his captain's summons to be served up his coffee and pastry.

Uncle had gotten no farther. He had written to say how sorry he was that we could not meet in San Francisco, but there would be a time for that. Anyway, he said, he was sending the double-breasted; I should look great in it. How amazing that all these sentiments could be conveyed in a postcard; the *Watsonville Mariner*, in color, held her bow proudly awash against the feathery crimson of a Pacific sunset.

This was the juncture when the man announced he must take me to his brother, who was a tailor. It was a fortunate coincidence that, in a matter of minutes, we could get there. He'd have me outfitted right.

"But I do not need any clothes," I protested.

"Something warm . . . that's what you must have."

"No, I do not need any," I insisted.

"You forget that clothes make the man!"

He was indefatigable. We had left the bridge and now the flow of traffic took us into a narrow and bustling street. My anxiety mounted. It's here he'll do it! Even without benefit of the watery depths, or of shadows, or of darkness. Scenes of this kind abound in Hollywood movies.

"My brother's shop is only two blocks away from here."

But I seemed to be merely imagining these words. For things around seemed to have come to a standstill. In the street nothing moved; the buildings to the left and right of us stood square-shouldered in a frieze of concrete, glass, and graying sunlight.

Were it not for several quick flashes of red that crossed my line of vision, I would not have understood that we had stopped at yet another traffic light.

"I've this train to catch," I heard myself speaking.

The old man remained quiet and remote now. Only his hands and shoulders moved, as we rejoined the traffic.

What would come next I had not the slightest notion. Never once during the next few minutes did I drop my guard. One false gesture and I might have swung the cab door open and run to safety. I'd be among the pedestrians in the sidewalk and slipping into a crowded shop or escaping to freedom in some alley.

I began reading aloud the names of the streets we passed. This seemed to have created an impression on him of my level of alertness.

"Now, here we are!" I announced on seeing the railroad station at Townsend and Third.

He pulled up at the curb and let me go without a word.

1982

The Tomato Game

DEAR GREG,

You must believe me when I say that I've tried again and
again to write this story. The man remains vivid in my memory, alone in his clapboard shack in the middle of a Sacramento Valley tomato field. It is a particularly warm Sunday,
in the height of summer. Also, it is the year of my miserable lectureship at Transpacifica University, which caters to
the needs of such an industry. Well, it's all because of the
ethnic pot. A certain number of offerings oriented toward
the minorities, and the university becomes entitled to certain funds. You have read in the papers how Transpacifica
gave an *honoris causa* to a certain personage—a prestigious
thing to do—which is that, indeed. Look up the word in the
dictionary; I do mean what I say. But to return to that summer when, in a fit of nostalgia, I had agreed to go with Sopi
(you must know him, of course) to look up some countrymen who might be into the national pastime of cockfighting.
It is illegal here, hence a *San Francisco Chronicle* headline—
"Transpacifica Lecturer in Bloody Bird Tourney Raid"—did
not seem at all unlikely.

We risked it anyhow and got much more. As in myth, the
signs were all over: the wooden bridge; the fork of the road;
the large track all around us which earlier had been a tomato
field; the harvesting machine to one side of the field, a men-
acing hulk, indicating how rich the crop had been—You can
see how hard I try. Would that I could have it in me to put all
this together.

I can tell you at this juncture that Alice and her young

man must be somewhere here in America. So is the old man, I'm positive. The likes of him endure.

"To such a man," Sopi said to me afterwards, "pride is of the essence. He is the kind who tells himself and his friends that as soon as he is able—in twenty, thirty years, say—he will return to the Islands to get himself a bride. How can you begrudge him that?" But it's the sort of talk that makes me angry, and at that time I certainly was.

I am now embarrassed, though, over how we behaved at the shack. We could have warned the old man. We could have told him what we felt. Instead, we teased him.

"Look, *lolo*," Sopi said. "Everything's ready, eh?"

For, true enough, he had furnished the clapboard shack with a brand-new bed, a refrigerator, a washing machine— an absurdity multiplied many times over by the presence, Sopi had noticed earlier, of a blue Ford coupe in the yard. "That's for her . . ." Sopi had said.

We enjoyed the old man immensely. He didn't take offense —no, the old man didn't. "I've been in this all along, since the start. Didn't I make the best deal possible, lolo?"

"Ya, Attorney," the old man said.

"He could have stayed in Manila for a while, lived with her, made friends with her at least," Sopi turned to me as if to tell me to keep my eyes off the double bed. The flower designs on the headboard were tooled on gleaming brass. "But his visa was up. He just had to be back. Wasn't that the case, lolo?"

"Ya, Attorney. Nothing there any more for me," the old man said.

"And this taxi-driver boy, is he coming over too?"

Sopi, of course, knew that the boy was—bag and baggage, you might say.

"That was the agreement," the old man said. "I send him to school—like my son."

"You know, lolo, that that will never do. He's young, he's healthy. Handsome, too."

"You thinking of Alice?" the old man asked.

"She's twenty-three," Sopi reminded him. I figured the old man was easily forty or forty-five years her senior.

"Alice, she's okay. Alice she is good girl," said the old man. "That Tony-boy . . . he's bright boy."

As an outsider, I felt uneasy enough. But the old man's eyes shown with fatherly satisfaction. There was no mistaking it. Wrong of you, I said to myself, to have cocksure ideas about human nature.

I saw Sopi in the mirror of my prejudices. He was thin but spry, and he affected rather successfully the groovy appearance of a professional, accepted well enough in the community and, at that, with deserved sympathy. Legal restrictions required that he pass the California Bar before admission to the practice of law amongst his countrymen. Hence, the invention which he called Montalban Import-Export. In the context of our mores he was the right person for the job the old man wanted done. Alice was Sopi's handiwork in a real sense, and at no cost whatsoever. Enough, Sopi explained to me, that you put yourself in the service of your fellows. I believed him. He knew all the lines, all the cliches.

I could feel annoyance, then anger, welling up inside me. Then, suddenly, for an entire minute at least, nothing on earth could have been more detestable than this creature I had known by the tag "Sopi." Sophio Arimuhanan, Attorney-at-Law, Importer-Exporter (parenthetically) of Brides—and, double parenthesis please, of brides who cuckolded their husbands right from the start. In this instance, the husband in question was actually a Social Security number, a monthly check, an airline ticket.

And I was angry because I couldn't say all this, because even if that were possible it would be out of place. I didn't have the right; I didn't even understand what the issues were. I was to know about the matter of pride later, later. And Sopi had to explain. It was galling to have him do that.

But at that moment I didn't realize he had been saying something else to me. "This Alice—she's a hairdresser. She'll be a success here. Easily. You know where we found her? Remember? Where did we find her, lolo?"

The old man remembered, and his eyes were smiling.

"In Central Market. You know those stalls. If you happen to be off guard, you can get pulled away from the sidewalk and dragged into some shop for a—what do you call it here?—a blow job!"

The old man smiled, as if to say, "I know, I know . . ."

"We tried to look up her people afterwards. Not that this was necessary. She's of age. But we did look anyway. She had no people any more to worry over, it turned out," Sopi went on. "She did have somebody who claimed to be an aunt, or something—sold tripe and liver at the meat section. She wanted some money, didn't she, lolo?"

"Ya, ya," the old man said. "All they ask money. Everyone." And there must have been something exhausting about recalling all that. I saw a cloud of weariness pass over his face.

"But we fixed that, didn't we?"

"Ya, ya," said the old man.

"Then there was the young man. A real obstacle, this taxi-driver boy. Tony by name," Sopi turned to me, as if to suggest that I had not truly appreciated the role he played. "We knew Tony only from the photograph Alice carried around in her purse. But he was as good as present in the flesh all the time.

The way Alice insisted that the old man take him on as a nephew; and I had to get the papers through. Quite a hassle, that part. It's all over now; isn't it, lolo?"

"Ya, ya," said the old man. "I owe nothing now to nobody. A thousand dollars that was, no?"

"A thousand three hundred," said Sopi. "What's happened? You've forgotten!"

"You short by three hundred? I get check book. You wait," said the old man.

"There's where he keeps all his money" Sopi said to me.

He meant the old bureau, a Salvation Army piece against the clapboard wall. Obviously Sopi knew the old man in and out.

"No need for that, lolo. It's all paid for," he said.

The old man's eyes brightened again. "I remember now!"

"Every cent went where it should go," Sopi said to me.

"I believe you."

"So what does her last letter say?"

"They have ticket already. They come any day now," the old man said.

"You'll meet them at the airport?"

"Ya."

"You've a school in mind for Tony-boy?"

And hardly had I asked then when regrets overwhelmed me. I should know about schools. The Immigration Service had not exactly left Transpacifica alone, and for reasons not hard to find. They had a package deal out there that had accounted for quite a few Southeast Asian, South Vietnamese, and Singaporean students. Filipinos, too. Visa and tuition seemed workable as a combination that some people knew about. A select few. It was a shame, merely thinking of the scheme. But, strangely enough, my anger had subsided.

"Ya," the old man said. Tony had a school already.

"That's why I wanted you to meet the old man," Sopi said. "Help might be needed in that area—sometime. Who can say?"

"You don't mean Transpacifica, do you?"

"That's your school . . . right?"

"How so?" I asked.

"Eight hundred dollars a year is what the package costs. The old man paid that in advance. It's no school, as you know."

"I only work there. It's not my school," I said.

"All right, all right," Sopi said. "There's all that money, and paid in advance, too . . . so this 'nephew,' bogus though he might be, can come over. You understand. We're all in this."

I began to feel terrible. I wanted to leave the shack and run to the field outside, to the tomatoes that the huge harvesting machine had left rotting on the ground. The smell of ketchup rose from the very earth. If it did not reach the shack, the reason was the wind carried it off elsewhere.

"Ya, they here soon," the old man was saying. "Tomorrow maybe I get telegram. Alice here, it'll say. Tony, too. You know I like that boy. A good boy, this Tony. Alice . . . me not too sure. But maybe this Tony, a lawyer like you some day. Make plenty money like you," said the old man to Sopi.

"Or like him," said Sopi, pointing to me. "Make much-much more, plenty-plenty . . ."

The old man seemed overjoyed by the prospect, and I had a sinking feeling in the pit of my stomach. The old man had trusted Sopi all along, and you couldn't but believe that he had seen enough models of Tony before.

We had come that Sunday, as I started to tell you, to see if we could watch a cockfight. When we left the shack finally,

Sopi said to me, "To think that that old man hasn't even met the boy."

As we drove down the road toward the fork that led to the wooden bridge, the smell of ripe tomatoes kept trailing us. That huge machine had made a poor job of gathering the harvest; and so here, Greg, is perhaps the message.

BESTS. . . .

1972

In the Twilight

THE SIGN SAID "MARYLOU'S EUROPEAN PASTRIES," and as we took a table and ordered coffee and croissants it was clear we were eight thousand miles and thirty years away from Panay. All the same, it was twilight once more in the barrio by the river, the quiet only occasionally broken by the shriek of a kingfisher and the splashing of tarpons feeding in the stream.

It was there we took refuge during the last days of the war, as I'd let on when asked, adding of course a detail or two, depending on my mood.

When the guerrillas brought in the prisoner, it was already late in the afternoon. They took over the barrio schoolhouse, as they always did. What would be the fellow's fate? From where we were, on our side of the river, we could hear the guerrillas laughing and singing. Off and on like that; it was weird. Major Godo's men they were, all right. Soon they'd even send for all the barrio girls—frightening the mothers, to be sure. What? A *baile*? Even at this time? Yes, why not? What was wrong with a bit of merrymaking? And they'd send for me, too.

They'd call from across the river: "Music! Hey, you there! Mr. Music! How about some music, Mr. Music?"

For in those days I could do things with the violin. And you just couldn't say, My strings snapped! or, My bow's broken!—no one would believe that, knowing how you wouldn't let things like that happen.

So we had an early supper. It'd be best to get ready.

I thought I heard them calling; but no, something had gone wrong. Dark began to set in, and we went to the river bank and sat there, wondering. What could Major Godo's men be up to now?

It was then that we heard the shot.

And this is what I told those who asked. That shot, I said, came from somewhere back of the schoolhouse, on the other side of the river.

In America, years later, the barrio vanished. Rightly so, you might say. But that shot—I heard it even better. I heard the echo clear through the swamps—across the years.

Now the Major was right there with us in the cafe, looking none the worse for wear, being past his mid-fifties, like Phil and myself.

"Drop that 'Major' business, please," he said.

He had had it easy under the new immigration law. He would become a U.S. citizen in three years, he told us proudly.

"Who could have imagined it then?" I said.

"I see an entirely new life ahead for you," Phil said, which was just like him to say.

"Yes, why not," I said.

"You both knew each other during the war?" asked Phil.

Long ago, in Manila, he had been Felipe Escondido, of the Ritz Music Makers. Now "Phil" seemed right; it suited the jazz piano player he had become. For that matter, I had become "Dan."

"Remember when we marched right into your barrio, in the middle of your fiesta?" asked the Major.

"You visited with us twice, Major," I said, catching the mistake too late, though.

"Quit it, will you?"

"Did Dan here already play the sax then?"

I suspected he was pleased we were safely employed,

having become union card–holders and all that. The Major had, for all his luck, still that far to go.

"As Godo here will tell you," I turned to Phil, "it was the violin then. The second time he and his men turned up, they had this prisoner with them."

"Dan remembers vividly how that one died," Phil said.

He, perhaps more often than the others, had asked me about the war. Now, with the Major there, he would know how true my stories had been.

"You couldn't possibly forget that shot . . . if you heard it at all," I said.

"I was supposed to do it," the Major said. "But I couldn't . . . I just couldn't. We had this messenger from San Paulino with the order . . ."

"So, then, who did it?"

Phil was anxious to hear the Major's version.

"Go ahead. You can tell him, if anyone can," I said.

"If you remember," the Major said, "one of the men I had was a fellow named Pungkol."

"The guitar player."

"If you remember, he had only one ear. On a dare he had trimmed off the other himself. That's how he got his name Pungkol. In San Jose it happened. The men had been drinking and someone had said, could this fellow prove he was braver than all the others."

Before I could put in a word, Phil said, "Oh, no!" In his shock, he had turned pale almost all at once.

"He had that switch blade always with him, and it was the same one he used there, back of the schoolhouse," the Major said.

"It wasn't you then?"

"Definitely."

"Which shot, then, was that one we heard?"

"You heard nothing, nothing at all. I couldn't do it. I

walked away, wetting my pants." He smiled, remembering. "The messenger saw, and I didn't like the look on his face and so gave him a blow."

By this time the coffee was cold in our cups.

"You didn't hear anything," the Major continued. "Pung-kol did it with his knife, touching the blade afterwards with his tongue, as if to say that even that . . . that, too . . . he could do. But, afterwards, he kept spitting for days on end . . . this way, this way . . ."

Phil covered his face, unwilling to see.

All this was thirty years away, and the croissants on the table looked like wave-washed seashells.

The Major left for his evening shift at Union Carbide, where he worked for Security.

"You two are simply lucky, having gotten to this country earlier," he said. "But this job's only temporary," he said, as if rationalizing. He would not be one to lose hope in somehow making it in his adopted country.

"How do you suppose you can play the sax tonight?" Phil asked.

I had to think for a moment. "No problem," I said—work is work, as they say.

"Keep remembering it was a shot you heard," he said.

"Whoever said it wasn't? *Because over the years it has been that. Nothing can change that. Nothing must.*"

We waited for a while outside Marylou's European Pastries for Phil's ride; then a car stopped in front of us. The door opened, and Phil's wife said to me, "Hi!"

"Hi!" I said also, thinking about nothing.

Anyhow, we were now as far away from Panay as anyone could get.

1978

The Gecko and the Mermaid

THE RAIN DECIDED WHAT HE COULD DO THAT SUNDAY.

"You call a taxi if you want," his cousin suggested, her tone indicating that she'd prefer staying home instead. "The nearest church is three blocks away."

But one look at the rain and he thought he'd better not risk a cold. He had his paper, "Patterns of Deception in Philippine-American Relations," to read at Palmer House the next morning. He was sixty-eight and lately had become overly careful about his health. Also, he had begun to take his membership in the community of U.S.-based Filipino scholars rather too self-consciously; he couldn't help it if he tried.

At breakfast, she had plied him with bran and raisins, toasted bread, two eggs over easy, and two slices of fried bacon, only to exclaim in horror that that was too much cholesterol, she was awfully sorry.

"But it's all right; it really doesn't matter," he assured her.

For being careful with food was a different matter altogether; it brought out the faddist in him. To indulge was, in this instance, to feel at home, to say that here was family.

As a college student she had stayed with his family in Quezon City. She was the extra place at the table, the third bed in the already crowded bedroom, with his two teenaged girls. A strain, all told. But there at the university you observed a vow of poverty; you broke it only when the gods decided to send some luck your way. In his case the gods gave him an opportunity to teach at Northridge, where, in an access of optimism, a Philippine Studies program had been started.

As for his cousin, relief came upon her winning a Catholic Women's League scholarship. Her apostasy surfaced, but there were Sisters around who mercifully wouldn't let her go and tactfully stood by. In Los Angeles, where her studies took her, there were the Good Shepherd Sisters, and in San Luis Obispo, the California Sisters of the Precious Blood. In short, they just didn't give up on her. Here in Chicago, she became close to the Sisters at the Mother Cabrini House. Now, if only her father had not passed on, and if only her mother and sister in the Philippines did not need the modest allowance she sent them. The idea was that she herself might join an order one of these days, be a Maryknoll Missionary perhaps, or a Sister with the Medical Missions somewhere in Pare, in Indonesia. In a way, her remaining in America had become a mission itself; for she had vowed that she would keep her sister and mother at home as well-provided as possible. She was forty-five now; her position at Barclay's was permanent, and it assured her a modest pension upon retirement. She'd then join her mother and sister in the Philippines. All she had to do for now was keep her mother in "Burpee's Seeds." Roses particularly were what her mother liked to grow; she had already seventeen varieties of them.

"Poor mother, she wants me back home, of course," she said. "She thinks I'm miserable here. But, as you can see, I'm well enough settled, even modestly happy, don't you think?"

"Didn't you once write, though, that there's a synagogue right next door?" he said, becoming somewhat uncomfortable with being asked to make an assessment.

She poured him his second cup of coffee. "It's good Maragugipe, from Guatemala. An office-mate from there gave me a pound yesterday. We have several Guatemalans in the office. In many ways, they're like us; they're all trying to come to America. You asked about the synagogue next door. I almost moved five months ago. You must have read about the anti-Jewish riots here. What if someone should bomb the place? This thought crossed my mind more than once, I assure you. But, in the end, I decided to stay."

He wondered what she meant by suggesting that danger lurked next door. Her apartment door, in full view across the breakfast table from him, had been fitted with a considerable amount of hardware.

"I had to call in a locksmith three months ago."

"You have . . . let's count! . . . two dead bolts, two padlocks, and a long chain. How long does it take to lock up when you leave for work or turn in for the night?"

"Five minutes."

"People might think you keep gold bars in here."

"Oh, let them. See all these keys!" She had brought out the bunch from her jeans pocket.

"What a nuisance!"

"Not when you've already lost a 19-inch Zenith TV. Oh no. That was on a Sunday morning, too. Just like today."

"Maybe, you're right. I read about those three Filipino nurses, too. Murdered by some nut, and right in their dormitory beds."

"Scares the hell out of you. Where can one go, really?"

He had stood up and paused by the living-room window.

"That's the lake out there," she said, observing that directly in his line of sight was a retaining wall, against which stood a grove of trees with strips of water in between. The newspaper article had described the place vividly. In the vicinity was the notorious Walpert Underpass, now off limits to joggers: there had been too frequent muggings there.

He had raised the blinds to better study the scene. Blobs of light with an eerie glow could be seen through the veil of rain.

"There's that fellow drowned there last year, you know. You read about that, of course."

"Wasn't that a suicide? He had brought his two little girls along, too."

"For three years it had been his wife, a dental assistant, who alone could hold down a job. It got simply too much for him."

"It would be, for oh so many," he said. "I can't help wondering why we are here in America. Why we come, in the first place. And why we stay."

"The Sisters come often, though," she said, as if anticipating his trend of thought. "These are from the Mother Cabrini House. In fact, they'll be here this afternoon. I told them about you, and they said they'll come and cook dinner for you. There are three of them, all from Iloilo, your father's home province."

"Very nice of them. Did they plan doing a special Ilongo dish?"

"I haven't the slightest idea. In any case, I asked my Guatemalan friends to come along too."

Eventually, their conversation turned to Buenavista, their hometown. Upon her father's death, she had resolved to venture forth and that was how she won the scholarship. She used to be terribly homesick, but she had gotten over it somehow.

"You know, I've not told this to anyone," he said, "but my debt to your father is boundless."

She propped her cheeks with her two hands. To one side, on the table, was a vase with some chrysanthemums. He moved this a few inches to one side so as not to block her face.

"Right this moment, you're your mother's spitting image. I remember so well how she looked as your father's bride. She lived then across the street from Uncle Rod and Auntie Delia. As a grade-schooler, it was with them I stayed. The house was our grandfather's anyway, Mother said. We were not imposing on them. I was nine then, and neither boarder nor househelp, only nephew to the elementary school headteacher and his wife, a boy from the barrio, at that. I scrubbed floors, ran to the bakery for *pan de sal,* ran to the Chinese store at the corner for coffee and sugar—errands like that.

"Your father would spend evenings with us. He was then with the National Guards, and quite a handsome figure he cut in his khaki uniform. Often he'd send me to the Chinese store for beer and cigars, which he took to your house across the street, to share with your mother's father. He was corporal in the constabulary."

"No. Sergeant," she said.

"The beer and the cigars must have failed to do the trick, for your father and mother took matters in their hands and eloped. For a long time I did not see your father. And then there was that one evening when he accosted me in the street.

" 'What's that thing you're hiding from me?' he demanded.

"With a firm grip on my shoulder he had made me do a ninety-degree turn. We were several yards away from the lamppost, though not for long, for he steered me to where it was light enough. It was impossible much longer to keep what I was holding out of his sight.

" 'What? A chamber pot?' he said, outraged.

"It had its lid on, of course. I had just returned from Subaan River where, earlier, I had dumped its contents and, in the rush of the flowing stream, got its bowl cleaned. 'Use your feet,' my aunt used to say; but I could never bring myself to try it that way.

" 'Your mother and father should hear about this. And to think you're in grade six now.'

" 'Grade seven,' I corrected him. 'I skipped sixth.'

" 'You did!' Your father was proud of me.

"He allowed me to proceed some ten steps ahead of him. When we reached the house, he came abreast of me and put his hand on my shoulder, a gesture I did not expect. Nor did I expect the kindness in his words, as he said: 'In that case, it's in high school you'll be next year.'

"And I don't know what happened, but the pot dropped at his feet . . . on his shoes, the lid breaking away . . . making quite a clatter, a calamitous embarrassment, even in that half-darkness by the housesteps.

"I must tell you that even now our hometown is not famous for sanitation . . . no town is! We are so backward still. In those days, there were hired men with hand-carts on which to load up pails collected from house after house. The method had the blessings of the town council, which outdid itself by designating a place somewhere in the harbor as the official waste disposal dump. To have a chamber pot of one's own was a sign of status, you'd better believe it. As to the lower orders, they had tacit access to the river, a section of which, in fact, had been provided with a concrete embankment . . . I am trying to be as vivid as I can. Does this make you sick?" he asked, for she looked quite troubled.

"Not at all. Go on," she said.

"And this I must add: after that meeting with your father, I made sure I did my chore after suppertime, under some cover of darkness. Your house, you might remember, had a large window facing the street, and it had capiz shell shutters. I could tell when your father was there a-courting; that window would be closed. In any event, I knew when it was that one could set out for Subaan. The capiz shells of the window shutters caught some streaks of light from the street lamps, rather enough to go by.

"So your father raised quite a row. Within a week, Mother dispatched Father to town and had me board with a copra merchant's family. This house was on Rizal Street. 'He's too small for his age, and his schoolbag so full of books . . . Better that he lives close to school.' This was how Father put it. The merchant would receive, instead of cash, Father's quarterly harvest of copra, never mind what the price in the market happened to be. Just keep away from Subaan River, Father made me promise.

"For four years, until after I finished high school, you couldn't have seen me anywhere near the Subaan house that was our grandfather's—Now do you see? Don't I owe your father a great debt?"

"I never knew this," she said, after a pause. "How could I possibly . . ."

"In the copra merchant's house, other boys from the outlying towns boarded as well. I remember the parlor so well. On one wall were pictures of the merchants' sons, nephews, and nieces in their graduation gear; on another, diplomas and certificates, in fancy glass-covered frames. It was quite a gallery, a testament to entrepreneurship, to buying and selling copra."

She appreciated the comment, responding with a wry smile.

"I've worked my way since high school, as you know. I've sold magazine subscriptions and hustled Americans at the Manila Hotel lobby with a pitch for a ten-volume encyclopedia entitled *Masters of Fortune*. Once I was dragged away by secret-service people. 'Didn't you know that that was High Commissioner Paul V. McNutt?' a bellhop confronted me, accusing me of violating the privacy of so high a personage.

"And ten years later, as a newspaper reporter now, I covered Mr. Quezon's election campaign for the senate. I was a Malacanang reporter in Manuel L. Roxas's time, which was about when America got Clark Air Force Base, remember?"

"You should write an autobiography, *manong*," she said.

"And call it what? 'From Chamber Pot to Typewriter'?" he laughed. "Although, come to think of it, it figures! Remember how much mileage the newspapers got out of President Quirino's fabulous bed and chamber pot?"

On that historical note he might have ended, but he remembered something. She reached for the vase of chrysanthemums and fiddled with the arrangement, to dissemble her own mood, perhaps. For his part, it came unbidden. "And, oh, there was something else," he said.

"Besides my father?" she asked.

He replied: "I'm thinking of the gecko. Come twilight, as you know, he taps several times on the palm frond or tree trunk. If something's troubling you, it's to him you turn. You listen as he taps on the palm frond. 'Gecko!' he calls out to you, in that sad but deep and resonant voice of his. At his first call, you say to yourself . . . supposing, for example, that you've been wondering all week long when Father might come to town . . . you'd say then, 'Father's coming.' 'Geeccckkkooo!' next comes his second call, and you say to yourself: 'Ah, Father isn't coming . . .' And comes the third call, a weak and faint one this time: 'Geeecccckk-koooo!' and you say to yourself again, 'Father's coming after all . . .' It's that way, only each call gets weaker and fainter than the one preceding, and then the intervals come longer and longer. Then, finally, you have only the silence of early evening . . ."

"You believe all that! And you still remember?"

"I do! I still do! How I used to strain my ears so as not to miss the gecko's answer. He lived in a palm tree on the opposite bank of the river. To empty the pot you have to bring it down to the water, bending carefully over the side of the embankment. I don't know how it happened, I must have gotten so distracted, my grip on the handle wasn't simply good enough. It was as if the water wrenched the pot from me, and down it tumbled among the rocks. But for a mound of debris and earth several feet away, blocking its escape downstream, I could have lost it altogether."

"What was it that troubled you then? What did you want to know from the gecko at that time?" she asked.

He wanted to laugh, recalling the scene by the darkening riverbank, but he was shocked by his failure of memory. A silence came upon him; it seemed he could hear the gecko again, his tapping against the palm frond yet a new readiness to answer another question. And what did he have now in his mind?

A chill ran down the small of his back.

At lunch time, she said: "We should expect the Sisters about two or three o'clock. Time enough for any writing or reading you need to do."

"I'm ready enough for tomorrow. Let me listen to some of your records instead," he said. "The burglars didn't find your stereo interesting, I see." He laughed.

"Try some folk songs. And that reminds me," she said. "Subaan River's where a mermaid lived. On some nights you might have heard her singing."

"So you remember that, too?"

"But, of course, I do! Perhaps, she might have . . ."

"What could a mermaid do with a nine-year-old?"

"She might have lured you and taken you to the depths of the river."

"Oh, no! I had no such luck."

"Well, then, this explains your leaving home and coming to America," she said.

"Those Guatemalans . . . do they like our folk music, too?" he asked, fitting a record onto the turntable.

1988

A Shelter
of Bamboo and Sand

ONE DAY IN NOVEMBER 1941, AN ACCIDENT BEFELL the young man Greg Padua. It was one of those things that should not have happened, especially in the presence of the girl with whom he was in love. He fell off the steps. It seemed that putting your feet where they should be was not quite enough. Other roles were destined for them.

Mr. Hidalgo himself had built the steps. To provide quick access, he said, proudly, to the air-raid shelter that he had dug, five feet below his back porch. He had paid no attention to the blueprints that Greg gave him some weeks back.

For the seven-by-ten-foot pit he needed, he had hired two laborers. He had it roofed up with bamboo flattened out into a wide mat. The men piled on top of this several bags of sand. From his collection of san franciscos, mayanas, daisies, impatiens and the like, Mr. Hidalgo selected the healthiest-looking ones and arranged them in rows over the pit for camouflage. Indeed the moss-girded clay pots lent the effort a considerable credibility. Stella, however, called it "Papa's Folly." Before the family gathered at the foot of the steps, her father had declared: "My contribution to the war effort!" But the little drama was lost on Stella.

The Hidalgos occupied the second floor of a wood-frame house on Richmond Street, some four blocks from the university. Stella was a senior there, at the College of Home Economics; her sister Helen, a junior at the University High School. And this was a good three weeks yet before Pearl Harbor . . .

Mr. Hidalgo was Records Division head of the Civil Service Bureau. Never had it entered his mind that some day he could be appointed director. He was pleased where he was. This war-to-be was America's war. When giants wrestle, the grass gets trampled, and you are wise to get out of the way. Mr. Hidalgo figured, though, that there was not much you could do if the contestants brought their wrestling right up on your lawn. No house on Richmond Street had one. A blessing! Mr. Hidalgo believed that it seemed fated they would be out of harm's way.

Feeling the way he did, discussing the news with the young man who, lately, had been escorting Stella home from her early Wednesday evening classes at the university, was pleasant. Stella and Greg would arrive right about supper time. This required the Hidalgos to set food aside for their college girl, who seemed never quite able to let her friend go. Well, they let that be. She'd just have to have her supper later, that was all. And more often than not, the young man seemed hardly eager to leave either.

Something had to be evolved to suggest that his time was up. Mr. Hidalgo did not let on that there was a problem, but quite by chance he missed his paper one evening. There followed a frantic five-minute search, with both his daughters Helen and Stella participating. Mrs. Hidalgo, an otherwise retiring figure, content enough to remain in the background, couldn't help reminding the girls that there is a well-loved Tagalog proverb which says "Whatever is lost is, of course, only too eager to find him who has been searching for it!" The girls eventually did find the paper: it was in the magazine stand to the left of the end of the sofa where Mr. Hidalgo himself had been sitting when Greg and Stella arrived. He had joined Mrs. Hidalgo in the dining room shortly, leaving the sofa free. It was there the young man was seated just a while back, and so Stella now said, "But, Papa, the *Standard*'s been here all this time!" and Mr. Hidalgo, dissembling his objective, "But, of course, how can I be so forgetful! In any event, what's in the news?"—turning to the young man in earnest.

Mr. Hidalgo found other methods of making the young man know when his welcome had worn out, but after not seeing the young man for three weeks or so, he would make up for it. Their discussions about the war would get more animated. Both had always been in agreement that it was already there except for the shooting, but the young man held out that, once started, it would take a long time ending. Mr. Hidalgo did not think so. The Americans would easily knock the Japanese cold. The latter had neither guns nor airplanes; their battleships were scraps of tin, leftovers from their toy-making days.

The family had been renters these many years, but from the way Mrs. Hidalgo did her homemaking, the impression created was that the Hidalgos owned their home. Appearances helped. Helen walked to school in her white blouse and pleated blue skirt; Stella, in whatever cotton frock the weather allowed. She made her own dresses (and her sister's, too), taking care not to look stylish or fashionable, to avoid being thought of as competing with college girls from affluent families.

Then came the nights with the practice blackouts. They had to be forthright about it: Greg must be sent on his way lest he be forced to wait out the long hour or two before "All Clear" sounded. Singalong, where he lived, could be reached simply by following the tramline. A cinch, even in the dark, he liked to say. But he recognized the wisdom of leaving early.

Then, one morning in late October, Stella announced at

lunch that she'd probably be late coming home that evening; the Home Economics Club, of which she was secretary,
would be entertaining the famous American writer Verne
Holland and his wife. There should be no cause for worry,
however. Greg would probably see her safely home.

"Probably?" asked Mr. Hidalgo.

"I mean he will, Father," said Stella.

"In the blackout?"

"Our party starts at four," said Stella. "It should be over
by six."

"Be home as early as possible then," said Mr. Hidalgo,
hiding his fears.

"Greg is all right, Father," said Stella.

The offices of the *National Sentinel*, where Greg worked,
were in Intramuros, near where the National Press Club
would set up its headquarters many years later. On the day
the Santo Domingo and the Ayuntamiento were both demol-
ished by Japanese bombs, the nondescript Sentinel Building
was spared a direct hit, but fire gutted it out of existence
anyhow.

Verne Holland and his wife Gwen Holland toured the
printing plant and chatted with Mr. Bollosos, the general
manager, in his office, a glass-paneled sort of cage where
goings-on, thus, were within view of everybody on the staff.
On any day the staff knew which of them received a dressing
down or worse.

Precarious though their hold on the job was, it had its
compensations. For Greg, there was the feeling of being in
the midst of things, in the sweep of events. The Verne Holland visit confirmed this. The author was a world-class celeb-
rity. For their copies of Verne Holland's immensely popular
novel, *Men Whom Gods Destroy*, the literati amongst Manilans
had queued up at the "Latest Fiction" counter of Philip-

pine Education Company. Accounts by certain Manila ladies about adaptations of certain love scenes in the novel began to appear thereafter in the society columns.

As fledgling writers hacking away at a pittance for Doble-posas Publications, Greg and his colleagues could only sur-mise what went on in the manager's cubicle with the Hol-lands there. The glass walls were like a movie screen of an Intramurous cine, in the days before the talkies, before the piano player in the pit had left his post to pee. But ah! said Greg to himself, what profound truths about art and life are being exchanged there, in air-conditioned comfort (the equipment was a novelty then). Only here, where you are, Greg said to himself, all you see is something in the nature of a mere pantomime. How unfortunate! And he diddled the upper-case key of his Underwood with his little fin-ger while conjuring the palaver between the famous couple and Mr. Bollosos. Actually, that is fame and fortune in the concrete right there, Greg thought. This very moment, the abstract has become concrete for me—and the idea elated him; he took a deep breath to let the access of exultation pass. No longer overwhelmed, a sad thought that his fel-low staff-members were pounding away at their typewriters possessed him. How so unaware his fellows were that some-thing memorable had just transpired, his recognition of it exacerbated by how his surroundings seemed to have now taken the better of him. The once all-too-familiar grind of the presses down in the basement, one floor below, turning out page upon page of the *Sentinel*'s noon edition, rocked the stuffy editorial room with a throbbing and scraping in a show of feigned diligence that seemed appropriate to threat-ened peons.

Greg remembered that day for yet another reason. Shortly

after the American writer's visit, a tall Negro came up to his desk.

"My invention," the man said triumphantly, depositing on Greg's cluttered desk an envelope containing blueprints for an air-raid shelter. He introduced himself as Mr. Norman. Could the *Sentinel*, perhaps, write it up? He felt he owed it to the Filipino people, he said, to have his blueprints available. "Look at my hand," he said. "Do you see my hand?" He pulled at his shirt sleeve so that the cuff rose a good two inches above his wrist.

"What's the point?" Greg wanted to ask, but thought better of it.

"My father fought at San Miguel de Mayumo," Mr. Norman continued. "He crept up to your people's lines and showed them his hand . . . this way." He held out an entire arm for Greg to admire, as it were. " 'We're brothers,' my father told your people; and they let him through. That's how he came to live in your country. I was born here. Now do you understand?"

Greg did; but the copy desk didn't. Sorry, guy, they told Greg. You've been had. What battle of San Miguel de Mayumo was your Norman talking about? Was there one, ever?

"But it's a sound idea," Greg protested. "All one needs is a hundred pesos worth of bamboo and a few sacks of sand! Don't you see what that means? He's already shown the Civil Air Defense people these plans!" He waved the blueprints like a flag. "I read the CAD endorsement, and . . ."

No one listened. The desk put Mr. Norman down as one of those cranks that the war hysteria appeared to have brought out of the woodwork.

But Greg took the blueprints with him when he went to

185

meet Stella that afternoon at the Practice House. Anything to serve as a topic of conversation between the old man and himself later on, he thought.

In the large parlor that hummed with three electric fans, a long table was richly laid: three varieties of noodles heaped on trays lined with glossy-green banana leaves; pink-and-blue portions of *sapin-sapin,* the platters in concentric circles; in one crystal bowl, mango punch, and in another, *guyabano* juice laced with *calamansi;* and, poised at each end of the table, gleaming silverware landlocked beside pitchers of tea and coffee, their complement of cups and saucers in proudly scattered islands.

Stella and her fellow club members made up a covey of young ladies in butterfly-sleeve dresses, their *panuelos* in green and gold, the college colors; during earlier occasions this get-up had always made an impression. They filed out to the porch to wait; a humid breeze laced about the acacia-lined walkway between the buildings. The girls brought out their fans, snapping them open with practiced movements so that the butterfly-sleeved blouses over their camisas would not later lack for stiffness.

It was some wait but the girls persevered, and at last their guests turned up, flanked by press photographers and sundry admirers.

At the *Sentinel* office, Greg had paid no attention to Verne Holland's loose linen suit nor to Gwen Holland's lavender dress of richly flowered chiffon, so winningly Hollywood-like in the now-admiring gaze, doubtless, of the Home Economic Club girls. In Mr. Bollosos's cubicle, the visitors had offered a sort of plantation look; it did not get through to the casual observer outside, perhaps because of the glass walls. But here, at the Home Economics Practice House, that colonial style demanded notice, for it belonged so fittingly; in fact, there was a seediness in the way both Mr. Holland and Mrs. Holland looked, almost as if this had been a calculated effect. Actually, it was perhaps just the effect of the weather, along with their having been diverted for courtesy's sake over to the Dean's for tea, and there compelled even to endure twenty minutes of chitchat with some faculty eager to show off the American English of their long lost U.S. campus days.

A polite food-tasting was about all that the Hollands could manage now at the Practice House, for the reason that several clerks at the Dean's office had already vied with one another for the honor of producing appropriate refreshments. And now, here at Practice House, there were more of the same. Gwen Holland tried eagerly to learn their names, charmingly repeating the native words as she was given them, and in this manner she scored well with the girls. They lusted for her autograph even more vigorously than for that of Mr. Holland. It now transpired that he was to be the Philippine Columbian Club dinner guest speaker within the hour. The Practice House stop had been a convenient detour.

Her duties over as member of the committee hosting the party, Stella sought out Greg at the first opportunity, for the offshoot of it all was that later a considerable amount of food had to be disposed of.

"How lucky can you get!" she said.

The remark was not intended to offend, but it could appear that way since Greg had come with several members of the university literary society.

They were boys his age although, unlike him, they were professional students. Instead of working at odd jobs, like clerking or proofreading or, as Greg did, dashing off feature stories, they hung about the Library Quadrangle. They called themselves Porch Lizards, claiming for their territory the steps of Palma Hall. To their left was the main reading room where an archway, with a Venus de Milo to one side and a Diana on the other, greeted the scholar with "Knowledge is Power" inscribed on marble. Everyone of course knew why the boys favored the spot: it afforded them the most generous of opportunities on campus for girl-watching.

Yes, Mr. Hidalgo remarked that there was no reason why Stella and Helen might not now see the shelter. It was late in the afternoon, but too early for anything to come up which might suggest to Greg—who happened to be visiting— that he might wish to leave soon. He sensed, in fact, that Mr. Hidalgo was pleased that he was there.

Helen could go first if she liked, Stella said.

"No, you first," said Helen, in turn—which Mrs. Hidalgo overheard in the kitchen. Anticipating that sooner or later she also would be asked, she came forward only to beg then and there to be excused.

Oh, but she should not forgo her "inspection rights," Mr. Hidalgo said.

"Some other time, maybe," she replied, perhaps feeling that something didn't seem right. "Thank you, anyway."

"You should see it, of course," Mr. Hidalgo turned to Greg finally. "It's not exactly what Mr. Norman's blueprints called for. I improvised," Mr. Hidalgo said proudly.

As twilight had set in, Helen was asked to fetch the lantern. She held it over Mr. Hidalgo's head as he made the descent, the rungs responding to his hundred and forty pounds with a rather immodest squeak.

Stella went next, unalarmed.

Helen's lantern lit up a circle of five or so feet in radius at the bottom of the steps. Mr. Hidalgo had led the way in, and it was from underneath the covered roof that he asked could Helen raise her lantern just so, to better light up the entry. Stella then could join him there below, Mr. Hidalgo said.

Stella did disappear into the shelter, as if magically, right before Greg's very eyes. He had remained at the back porch, among the potted san franciscos and mayanas, and from where he stood, he lost her for a while. When he saw her again, she had been reduced to the round of a shoulder and the curve of an elbow. But she was there in the shelter, all right; she was calling out to him.

"You have to see this to believe it!"

It was an invitation impossible to decline. Her father's might have been given him, Greg said to himself, out of politeness; this one was genuine.

Greg hovered over the first two rungs safely, but the third and fourth gave him trouble. The rattan strips that secured both rungs onto their notches had loosened up. Thrown off balance, he tried to steady himself but failed. Only by avoiding too much of a crash did he redeem himself somewhat. Even so, he elicited an anguished cry from Stella, who was just then emerging from the camouflaged pit below.

"Oh, Papa!"

Greg heard it distinctly. Already she was certain about whom to blame.

"Hurt?" she asked.

"Oh no, I'm not," he assured her, brushing off some dirt.

"But your trousers . . . look," she said.

"You got bruised?" Mr. Hidalgo asked. He had reached for the lantern and now was holding it only about a hand's-breadth away from Greg's face.

He felt his eyebrows were getting singed.

The area that the lantern illuminated included a large portion of Greg's right leg; a nail from somewhere had caught his trouser cloth. Not quite happy with that, it had also taken a small bite of flesh underneath.

Years later Greg discovered the notebook in which he had jotted down the incident. His companion and fellow wanderer through many a change of place and season, the notebook had been among odds and ends that had resisted disposal. It had held up well, ruled pages and all, to assert the import of this episode of his youth which had had for its setting a world on the verge of blowing up. How inexorably history had brought on death thereafter to peoples and nations, yet the words had remained. He had written in pencil, making no claim to finality. But they had been his words, and with them he had dared, although not meaning to, to challenge Time. His having written, however poorly or well, might be all that would live.

1988

The Long Harvest

ONE AFTERNOON IN SEPTEMBER, AS NONONG PADUA was hurrying home to his lodgings outside the North Gate, a gust of wind swept past him heavy with the smell of sunshine. He had just left the Hub and had come abreast of Padelford. For a graduate student in anthropology at the university, and expecting his master's the following year, it was an occurrence of no particular value, to be sure; but it disconcerted him, and only after some effort was he able to pull himself together. By then a whole squad of chipmunks had gathered at his feet and had begun making faces at him. In the past, he had always depended on their antics to amuse him; this time it was indifference that he had reserved for them, a feeling which, in any case, he hardly hoped to convey to the poor creatures.

But what if the chipmunks were meant to remind him of something? And what might that be? He couldn't think of anything—although, oh well, it could be some feeling he could not identify, a dead freight perhaps that needed accounting for, nothing more.

And then came a second gust, leaving a whirl of leaves skittering before him for several seconds or so. Then the smell of sunshine once more: it was unmistakable.

Mothers know it only too well. After hanging out for hours at the beach or riverbank, and having soaked in all that heat, boys head for home bringing not much else but that smell. "You remind me of Tia Martina's rice containers," his mother would tell him out of kindness, when in fact he reeked of the sun and tracked it in all over the place, his head like a basket of dried anchovies.

It was the year after he had arrived in America that he lost his mother. The Marcos regime had begun. Granting that no possible harm could befall him if he made a quick visit home, why risk it? What if something went wrong? Already the homeland was accommodating itself to the dictatorship. His return to the States could be in jeopardy. He had been lucky enough to win himself a scholarship, and there was no reason to give it up by allowing himself to get caught in the new web of authoritarianism. Thanks to the Funds for Third World Development, he could bide his time about returning. In imagined conversations with family members, each and everyone of them commended his decision. Have courage, they urged; in the meantime they would take care of themselves as best they could. He felt many a time the gentle touch of his mother's hand on his brow; he could stay abroad as long as he wished, the words of blessing lingering long. She was safe there in the barrio, where she and Father had started out years back then—did anyone care to remember? But that was not said in recrimination. It was right for him to go abroad, and he did not doubt that even as she breathed her last she forgave him his absence, his now nine years of exile. He let his book sack slip off his shoulder as he took the nearest bench. By then three crested blue jays had driven the chipmunks away, seemingly anxious to present a performance of their own: half-steps and leaps, with wings coquettishly spread, the tips quivering, their heads decorously favoring now a left, now a right turn. Towards what end he was in no position to surmise, for at this point he had only thoughts of home, his entire being quite overcome.

He recalled how, through exposure to the sun and the dew, *buri* leaves were prepared for weaving, how, when curing the raw leaves, great care was taken. The attention, in retrospect, was so out of proportion to what the material turned into. Stripped into strands of about the width of your fingernail, the fronds of the palm became mere rice-containers. This was in anticipation of *palay,* the unhusked rice that harvest might bring. There was never much of that, though; poor harvests were the rule rather than the exception.

One of the jays had shuffled forward and now, as if taking leave, made a deep bow before him and then darted away with two companions following, a dazzle of ruffled wings and twitter.

There were days when Tia Martina's yard was a sea of palm fronds. The leaves, when not yet severed, were merely opened fanwise upon the ground. All the same, they made the yard beautiful to behold, each frond displaying its own shade of green or yellow. What with the many nights of dew and mornings of bleaching in the sun, each frond lay afterward in splendor. Then the day for stripping, and now the yard bare. The boy's mother had put in an order for rice-containers, as many as the old weaver could make. The bags had to be the kind that could hold twenty-five *gantas* of unhusked rice, which meant they had to be five hand's-breadths in girth and seven in height, squared at the bottom. Tia Martina would receive twenty centavos for each. From the way his mother and Tia Martina discussed the project, you could say that rice-containers were their very life.

"Five are ready now, Nonong," the old woman told him.

Tia Martina had called him by the name that only the family used.

He watched her put the finishing touches on the last bag. Her fingers trembling, she fixed the alignment of a strip here and a fold there. Her thumb, seemingly the leader of a crew, bade the other fingers to patience and perseverance. Yes, yes, the knotted fore- and middle-fingers obeyed, giving up on those yet unhinged from the gnarled knuckles.

Then the old woman got up, the strips of buri leaves amidst which she had been sitting falling away at her feet. Their rustling was like that of quails bolting out of a hedge, startled.

Now with the heel of her palm she bore down heavily on the bags, straightening corners before folding them. The five would make a modest bundle for Nonong to bring home without difficulty.

With a length of hempen string, she tied up the batch. He observed how carefully she allowed some slack for easy holding.

"Tell your mother that the others will be coming, only I have not been feeling well," she said. "It's malaria. That's all . . ." But she said this as if the disease were a family member, a granddaughter, say, that had acquired wrong habits and was beyond reform, a bad seed. The chills used to come every third day; now they racked her daily. And promptly, too; right about mid-morning, ruining everything. "Can you tell your mother that?"

"Yes, I shall." It was the first time he had spoken. And he wanted to say more, but it felt as though something held him back.

It was time to leave. The barrio schoolhouse sat in the morning sun, its thatched roof humped in the middle of a bare playground. Earlier on, boys and girls had been running around; now it was empty.

He could have been in school, too, had Mr. Flores approved. But he was only five, and short and frail besides. For the listing, his mother took him to the schoolhouse herself.

"Oh, Mrs.," Mr. Flores greeted his mother.

"This boy can read and write already," she declared. "Are we going to let him wander around the village with nothing to do?" Mr. Padua, his father, had been teacher-in-charge only the year before, and there would have been no problem then. But he had left the school service for a homestead that he had staked out in Bondoc, in the interior.

"The boy . . . oh yes, the boy!" said Mr. Flores. "What a surprise, what an honor that you have come. Now, Mrs., what can I do for you?"—knowing all along what they had come for. "Well, let's see . . . Come this way, boy." And, presently, his hand on Nonong's shoulder: "Stand right here before me. Erect! Like a soldier!"

"Erect!" his mother repeated. "Like a soldier!"—her voice trembling.

"Feet close together," said Mr. Flores.

"Feet close together."

Grinning, Mr. Flores said, "Now try this," reaching his right ear with his left hand, elbow over his head. "Look, it's this way. Follow me."

Nonong let his right arm hang loose at his side for a moment. Then he raised his left, to test its stretch.

Oh, but how heavy his arm had become!

"Don't cheat!"

A sharp pain shot down the length of his arm. Mr. Flores had grabbed his elbow and pressed. It felt as if his middle finger could give him in an instant that extra inch, but he pitched forward instead.

"There, you see . . ." Mr. Flores exulted. "He simply can't make it yet . . . Rules are rules! I'm doing my best, Mrs."

"You and your rules!" his mother protested—his mother dragging him away and repeatedly shouting, "Don't you ever say the boy cheated!" until they had finally crossed the playground . . .

Nonong hoisted the bundle once more on his shoulder. The bags rubbed against his cheeks and some of the buri strips felt rough but after a while it did not matter anymore.

It seemed, in fact, as though petals of sunshine, if ever such things existed, had been slipped between the folds of the rice-containers. With a smile, he pressed the bundle against his head.

There had been a storm the night before, the first of the monsoon that year. The windward side of the village was *arumahan*, overgrown with the thorny cassia bush, the all-too-characteristic feature of the seashore in those parts. As the bush would grow into a windbreak against the south-wester, people allowed it to stay wild, although it gave the village the appearance of one soon to be abandoned. New paths to the high ground where the first huts were clustered had to be made, in place of the old ones strewn with thorny branches. Not quite threatened yet, although looking some-what hunkered there in the half-shade of the coconut grove, was the wood-frame house that was home to Nonong. And perhaps even more bravely hopeful was the quiet of morning itself with its touch of children's voices.

He came abreast of the school gate, and there was Mr. Flores, holding forth: " 'This is Pepe. This is Pilar. Here is Spot . . .' "

Tattered palm fronds from the last storm lay scattered every which way along his path. He made his way care-fully; he must not hurt himself before he could deliver Tia Martina's work.

From on top of a hump of one large frond something moved, and he caught his breath. It was a lizard, mottled green and gold, a whole foot in length, and aglow against the green of the coconut leaves.

It raised its head, as if in salute. Then it flicked its tail and slid away into a pile of leaves.

Nonong hurried homeward, dazed. A strong nauseating smell greeted him when he reached the steps, where his mother had been waiting. It came from a tin can of tar in her hand.

"For marking the bags," she said, showing him the dark, viscous stuff. "People these days can't keep their hands off things that don't belong to them."

Already she had a bamboo stick about a hand's-breadth long, a ready brush. He helped her lay the bags on the slatted floor, one atop the other.

The first bag flattened out easily before her, and his mother began working, dipping the stick. Nonong had to keep the container steady, using both his hands to hold it down.

"Watch!" she said.

She began with L, building the face of the letter one obdurate stroke after another. The golden-green of the buri strips easily took the tar. The letter required several strokes. Then she left it to dry and proceeded with the letter I, twirling the stick so as to catch a blob of tar about to drop onto a wrong spot.

But it was the right place after all. The new letter was slowly becoming a P. Once a flourish of his mother's wrist caught a black sliver of tar thinning down, and a second turn of the stick transformed it into a quivering thread.

"But those are the letters of my name!" Nonong said. His fascination wore off.

"And why not?" his mother chuckled.

A strange thing came over him. It was the tar; he had breathed in too much of it.

"The old woman, Ma," he began, afraid that nausea might get the better of him and keep him from delivering Tia Martina's message. "She has malaria. She told me to tell you."

"Is that what she said?" his mother asked, noticing something the matter with him.

He took a deep breath and said it as bravely as he could. "I'm sure, Ma. That is what she told me to tell you."

"And what did you say?"

"I promised to tell you."

She put her stick away. "Then go quickly, Nonong. Bring her some quinine tablets."

"Of course, Ma," he said.

And he caught his breath, for this was an errand unlike any in the past, although what he had in mind was not Tia Martina but the lizard—it would turn up again! He needed to see it again, mottled green and gold, aglow in the sun.

In time the arumahan claimed other villages, other shores.

1990

Glossary

The Philippine terms in each story appear for the first instance in *italics* and then afterwards in roman.

ABRASADOR. A leg pillow.

ADOBO. A stew of pork, chicken, beef or a combination of any two of these, or even of all three, featuring a generous use of garlic, pepper, and vinegar. It enjoys a reputation as the Philippine national dish.

AMIHAN. North wind.

ANAK. A little boy or girl, not necessarily one's own son or daughter.

AROMA. The thorny cassia bush of the coastal areas such as the mouth of rivers and beaches. A stretch of such growths is called the ARUMAHAN—literally, where the AROMA is thick—and, thus, is a welcome windbreak.

ASALTO. A surprise party.

BAILE. A dance party.

BANBAN. A variety of reed.

BATEL. The two-masted schooner.

BEJUCO. A climbing palm with long, slender stems; also known as *rattan*.

BURI. The talipot palm. Its leaves are stripped and woven into sleeping mats or rice-containers.

CALAMANSI. The fruit, from three-fourths to an inch in diameter, of a variety of citrus tree.

CAMISA. A blouse, usually loose and of cheap cotton material.

CARENDERIA. A wayside eating-place.

CARGADOR (CARGADORES, pl.). Porter.

CAVAN (CAVANES, CAVANS, pl.). A unit of measure for rice or corn, equivalent to 2.13 bushels.

CHUPA (CHUPAS, pl.). A measure for rice equivalent to one-eighth of a GANTA.

COIR. The fiber of the coconut husk, used for rope-making.

DAO. One of several commercially important cabinet woods with dark brown markings.

GANTA. A measure of rice or corn, equivalent to eight CHUPAS, or one twenty-fifth of a CAVAN.

GAPI. That phase in the preparation of a clearing, for rice or corn planting, that involves the systematic removal of burned material, tree stumps, and the like.

GUYABANO. The sour-sop tree.

HARAO. The equivalent of "Halt!" when a carabao is being brought to a stop. The word is Bisayan.

HINAGDONG. One of several quick-growing trees in areas that have been cleared for rice and corn planting.

KAINGIN. Land prepared by the slash-and-burn or swidden method.

KOGON. A variety of bamboo grass used for roofing.

LAMPARILLA. A small, crudely made kerosene lamp, or LAMPARA.

LANCHON. A one-masted boat still used for moving cargo from one riverain or seaside community to another, the end-of-the-line remnant of the boat-building industry in the days of the Spanish galleons.

LAUAN. The Philippine mahogany of the third-class variety.

LOLO. Grandfather, or any old man.

MANONG. Elder brother, or, simply, a prefix to use when addressing an older or a respected person.

MERIENDA. Mid-afternoon refreshments in the form of rice cakes and the like.

NANAY. Literally, mother; or, a form of address, or the substitute for the name of an older or respected woman.

NOROESTE. The northeast wind.

PALAY. The rice grain that is yet to be husked or milled; also rice still on the stalk.

PANUELO. Shawl.

PARAO. A dugout; also a sailing vessel with outriggers.

POBLACION. The town or townsite.

PRINCIPALIA. The well-to-do or so-called first families of the POBLACION.

ROSARIO. The rosary.

SALA. The living-room.

SAMPAGUITA. A variety of the jasmine, regarded as the Philippine national flower.

SAPIN-SAPIN. A blancmange of several colored layers, sweetened and flavored with coconut milk.

SIKOY-SIKOY. A gambling joint.

SUSMARIOSEP. Literally, "Jesus, Maria, Joseph!"

TATAY. Father; but, like NANAY, has become an all-purpose word when addressing the elderly.

TUBA. Toddy, or wine, from the coconut palm.

UBOD. The pith of a palm.